THE CRESTLINE SERIES

AMERICAN Beer Trucks

DONALD F. WOOD

MBI Publishing Company

Dedication

To Bill West

First published in 1999 by MBI Publishing Company, 729 Prospect Avenue, PO Box 1, Osceola, WI 54020-0001 USA

© Donald F. Wood, 1999

MBI Publishing Company books are also available at discounts in bulk quantity for industrial or sales-promotional use. For details write to Special Sales Manager at Motorbooks International Wholesalers & Distributors, 729 Prospect Avenue, Osceola, WI 54020-0001 USA.

Library of Congress Cataloging-in-Publication Data
Wood, Donald F.
   American beer trucks/Donald F. Wood.
      p. cm.—(Crestline series)
   Includes index.
   ISBN 0-7603-0440-8 (pbk.: alk. paper)
   1. Trucks—History. 2. Refrigerated trucks—History. 3. Beer—Transportation—United States—History. I. Title. II. Series.
TL230.5.B43W66   1999
629.224—dc21   99-11566

On the front cover: A trio of classic beer trucks, from the top: a 1963 GMC cab-over fitted with a Dailey body to transport Miller beer. *Dailey Body Company*; a 1934 White carrying barrels of Renners Old Oxford Ale, brewed in Youngstown, Ohio. *American Truck Historical Society*; and a 1941 Dodge fitted with a custom streamlined body.

On the back cover: A 1950 White carrying barrels of Golden Hudepohl beer. *American Truck Historical Society*; a driver unloading a wooden case of Hoosier beer from a 1933 Studebaker. *American Truck Historical Society*; and a 1969 GMC tractor with a Hesse 12-bay trailer transporting Budweiser. *Hesse Corporation*

Edited by Jack Savage
Designed by Katie Sonmor

Printed in the United States of America

Contents

	Acknowledgments	4
	Preface	5
	Introduction	6
Chapter 1	The Early Years of Motor Trucks and Electrics 1901–1910	8
Chapter 2	Gasoline Engine Trucks Gain Ground 1911–1920	13
Chapter 3	Prohibition Rules the Decade 1921–1930	28
Chapter 4	Happy Days Are Here Again 1931–1940	33
Chapter 5	Wartime Horsepower 1941–1950	77
Chapter 6	Distribution Goes National 1951–1960	99
Chapter 7	99 Bottles of Beer on the Truck 1961–1970	112
Chapter 8	Consolidation and Imports 1971–1980	121
Chapter 9	Big Trucks, Lite Beer, and Microbreweries 1981–Today	126
	Bibliography	143
	Index	144

Acknowledgments

I appreciate the help of many who assisted, and I hold them blameless for errors the book might contain. They include: Anheuser-Busch Archives; Peter Blum, Stroh Brewery Company; Bob Chant, LaBatt; Ralph Dunwoodie; Grace Ellis, Pabst Brewing Company; Charles Fontaine, Gambrinus Drivers Museum; Deanna Gallaway, Moosehead Breweries, Ltd.; Chris Hem, Red Hook Brewery; Bob Koprivica, Jr.; Ralph Kunkemoeller, Oldenberg Brewing Company; Michael Luke; Peter Maglathlin, The Danbury Mint; F. X. Matt II, Matt Brewing Company; David Norton; Teresa O'Donnell, Guinness Ireland Group; Bill Reiff, Hesse Inc.; Chuck Rhoads; Larry L. Scheef, American Truck Historical Society; Allan Shocker; Jay R. Troger, Hackney and Sons, Inc.; Art Van Aken; Jeff Waalkes, Miller Brewing Company; Charles Wacker; Mark Wayman; Bill West; and William J. Wright.

Several persons generously support a fund at San Francisco State University that supports old truck research, and I'd like to acknowledge some of the donors: Stuart B. Abraham, Phillip S. Baumgarten, Edward C. Couderc of Sausalito Moving & Storage, Gene Bills, Gilbert Hall, David Kiely, ROADSHOW, Gene Olson, Oshkosh Truck Foundation, Art Van Aken, Charlie Wacker, Bill West, and Fred Woods. Several chapters of the American Truck Historical Society have also provided financial support to the program at San Francisco State University. The chapters include Black Swamp, Central Coast of California, Hiawathaland, Inland Empire, Mason-Dixon, Metro Jersey, Minnesota Metro, Music City, Northeast Ohio, Shenandoah Valley, and Southern Michigan.

—*Donald F. Wood*
San Francisco State University

Preface

In researching this book, I was pleased to discover a photo, shown in the introduction, of the Fox Head Waukesha Corporation, brewers of Fox Head Beer, located just eight blocks north of where I lived as a boy in Waukesha, Wisconsin. Personal connections to history are often the most intriguing.

In selecting photos to be used in this book, I tried to use those associated with a wide variety of brews. Readers will note that many of the trucks pictured are Whites. As this book was just underway, the American Truck Historical Society, whose library includes the White photographic archives, offered to sell copies of beer truck photos, and a selection was made of pictures showing different brands of beer.

In a few instances I may err when identifying the name of a brew, and instead may be using the name of a distributor. Also, in the case of a few restored trucks, the name featured as a brand of beer may have been made up by the truck's restorer. There's also a chance that some of the brands we show were non-alcoholic, or "near-beers," at which a regular beer-drinker would scoff.

Introduction

Beer is a popular beverage with a European heritage. Long before the motor truck, beer kegs were distributed in horse-drawn wagons. Originally, most breweries were "local" in nature, and their beer was distributed within a short radius of the brewery.

Trucks replaced horses and allowed breweries to increase the distances the beer was transported. Beer was a heavy load, and trucks used in the trade tended to be heavy-duty. It was also necessary to keep the beer cool.

In the United States, Prohibition caused a large gap in the development of beer trucks. Sales of alcoholic beverages were illegal from 1920–1933. Some "near-beers" were sold during that time. During this span, truck chassis themselves underwent many technological and styling changes. Trucks of the late 'teens were square and boxy, had open cabs, and ran on solid tires. By 1933, trucks had enclosed cabs and pneumatic tires, and streamlining that was used for autos would shortly be applied to trucks.

Cases of bottled beers were carried in beverage bodies on shelves, usually enclosed inside doors that were kept locked. Larger customers began handling beer in pallet loads, and beverage trucks were designed with bays that opened to either side and were loaded and unloaded by forklift trucks.

While a few giant breweries presently dominate much of the nation's markets for beer, small "boutique" breweries are opening daily. Initially, they sell their product at their own bar, but some become sufficiently successful that they start distributing locally by truck.

Waukesha, Wisconsin's Fox Head beer was carried in this Fruehauf trailer pulled by a late-1930s White. In the rear one can see empty barrels moving down a chute. The author lived in Waukesha as a boy, about eight blocks south of the brewery shown here. *American Truck Historical Society*

Foreign beers are popular in the United States and a number of pictures are included of trucks used in their distribution in Canada and in Europe.

The beer truck body or trailer is manufactured by a firm separate from that of the chassis manufacturer. The beer distributor buys both the chassis and the body separately. The empty chassis is delivered to the body builder who fits and paints the body (or entire truck, if necessary) and attaches lettering and decals supplied by the breweries. Sometimes a body will be transferred from an older chassis to a new one.

A restored White Labatt's truck at the 1986 EXPO held in Vancouver, Canada. A Labatt's press release said when the company decided to restore a rig, three discarded trailers were found, but no tractor. This tractor had to be built from scratch.

This early-1950s picture was taken in front of the Miller's Miami distributor. The trucks are Chevrolets, the autos are Fords. *Miller Brewing Company*

The majority of beer trucks the author spotted while working on this book had Anheuser-Busch markings, such as this Bud Light truck with semitrailer spotted near Algoma, Wisconsin.

Chapter One

The Early Years of Motor Trucks and Electrics
1901–1910

The motor truck was introduced at about the turn of the century and its acceptance was slow. Railroads carried freight between cities, while horses pulling wagons were used for making local deliveries. Few pictures seem to have survived showing beer trucks in use during this decade.

Virtually all beer was distributed in barrels and kegs, although the automatic bottling machine had been invented in 1890 and, eventually, would have an impact on the distribution patterns of beer. Pasteurization, also a nineteenth-century discovery, would prove to be of significance to the production and distribution of beer. Unpasteurized beer must be protected from the sun, heat, and variations in temperature.

During this first decade of the new century, electric trucks had their brief moment of fame, and some were sold to breweries. Their short range was not an issue since they were compared with horses.

Horse-drawn wagons continued to be used. An old Pabst Brewing Company press release contained the statement that at one time the firm's stable contained 800 draft geldings, which were used to haul 250 to 300 beer wagons.

A 1904 Columbia electric truck, used by Anheuser-Busch, and featured in the truck builder's advertisement. Columbia trucks were made in Hartford, Connecticut from 1899 until 1907. *Charles Wacker*

RIGHT: A picture of the Anheuser-Busch city delivery depot in St. Louis. The truck on the left is probably a Walker Electric, while behind it are Columbia Electrics. Walkers were built in Chicago from 1906 until 1942. *Anheuser-Busch Archives*

Barrels of Miller High Life hauled by a wagon. Note that the word "Miller" is painted on the awning over the driver. *Miller Brewing Company*

A team of horses prepares to pull a load of cases of Miller's. *Miller Brewing Company*

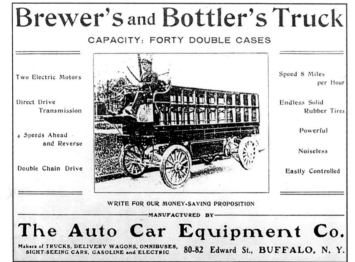

Brewer's and Bottler's Truck

CAPACITY: FORTY DOUBLE CASES

Two Electric Motors

Direct Drive Transmission

4 Speeds Ahead and Reverse

Double Chain Drive

Speed 8 Miles per Hour

Endless Solid Rubber Tires

Powerful

Noiseless

Easily Controlled

WRITE FOR OUR MONEY-SAVING PROPOSITION

MANUFACTURED BY

The Auto Car Equipment Co.

Makers of TRUCKS, DELIVERY WAGONS, OMNIBUSES, SIGHT-SEEING CARS, GASOLINE and ELECTRIC   80-82 Edward St., BUFFALO, N. Y.

The Auto-Car Equipment Co. of Buffalo advertised this "Brewer's and Bottler's electric truck, which could carry 40 double cases." *Charles Wacker*

The makers of Bavaria beer, which has been brewed in Holland for several centuries, use this horse-drawn cask for promotional purposes. *Bavaria*

Bavaria used this horse-drawn wagon, probably a replica, for promotional purposes. This one was spotted in downtown Amsterdam in 1997. Note the kegs dangling from chains at the rear of the wagon.

Kelly Springfield featured this Poth's Extra Beer electric truck in its tire ads.

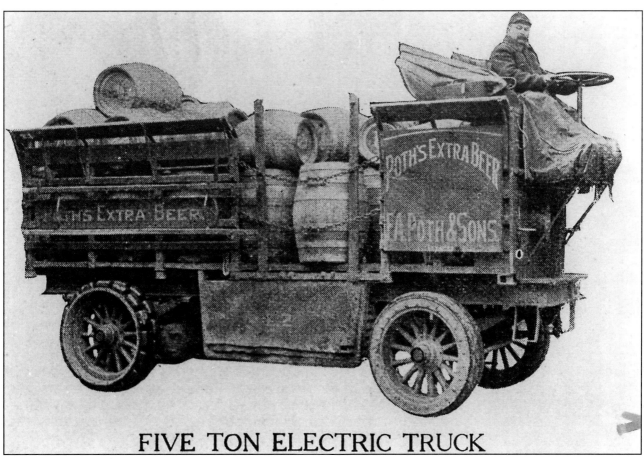

FIVE TON ELECTRIC TRUCK

"AMERICAN" CHASSIS WITH BREWERY BODY

An American truck carrying barrels of Lion beer. Several different firms built trucks with the "American" name. *Smithsonian Institution*

A 1910 Grabowsky loaded with empty barrels, and operated by the C. Pfeiffer Brewing Company. Grabowsky trucks were built in Detroit from 1908 until 1913 and are one of the ancestors of GMC trucks. Pfeiffer beer was brewed in Detroit. *National Automotive History Collection, Detroit Public Library*

A circa-1910 Alco operated by the Central Brewing Company, apparently in New York City. The American Locomotive Company built Alco trucks in Providence from 1909 until 1913. *Smithsonian Institution*

This unidentified make of truck was featured in a Tivoli Brewing Company ad in a 1910 Detroit newspaper. The ad's caption under the photo said, in part: "One of the many trucks now kept busy delivering Altes Lager Bier. Altes Lager is the beer you want. It is food and drink combined. A pint of Altes is a pint of health. Your doctor will recommend it. A case at your home (24 pints) . . . for $1.25." *Bill West*

Chapter Two

Gasoline Engine Trucks Gain Ground
1911–1920

For beer trucks, 1911–1921 was a short decade. They were introduced into use early, distributing barrels of beer and ale in local markets. Their main drops were of barrels and kegs to taverns that their respective breweries controlled. But by 1920 they were no longer needed as Prohibition supposedly ended the sale of beer (and other alcoholic beverages). Hundreds of breweries shut down, never to reopen. There was also a form of Prohibition in Canada that started during World War I and which lasted into the 1920s.

According to one study of the beer industry during this period, beer varied in flavor from locality to locality, not unlike the microbreweries of today. The publication noted that before Prohibition, only a few beers were known or distributed and the best known were Budweiser, Pabst Blue Ribbon, and Schlitz. Some ales, such as Smith's, Ballantine, Jones, and Foxhead, were brewed and distributed in local territories.

Most truck bodies in this era were built by one-time wagon builders, who would build a body and place it on a truck chassis. Anheuser-Busch had a wagon-building shop where they had originally built beer wagons for their own use and for their distributors. Those shops also turned out truck bodies as trucks replaced horses.

By as early as 1912, gasoline trucks were found to be superior to electric trucks in meeting the brewing industry's needs. A 1912 article said, "while the electric [truck] is holding its own on short radius hauls, it is entirely out of its class on long distances. Thus it happens that many breweries which started to experiment with small fleets of electrics and afterwards increased into big installations, have latterly begun to supplement

A 1911 Marquette with chain drive carrying Reisch beer in cases. Note the lamp on the side and at the rear. Marquette trucks were produced in Chicago from 1910 until 1912. There was a Reisch Brewing Company in Springfield, Illinois. *National Automotive History Collection, Detroit Public Library*

A 1911 Mack operated by the Wm. Peter Brewing Company of Union Hill, New Jersey. *Charles Wacker*

their transportation equipment with gasoline wagons for outlying territories."

The Anheuser-Busch motorized fleet at this time consisted of 24 passenger cars, 50 electric trucks, and ten gasoline trucks. Anheuser-Busch built a garage to house its fleet (the phrase the 1912 magazine used was "accommodations for stabling the motor wagons"). The facility included a four-vehicle wash rack, a 10,000 gallon underground gasoline tank (large enough to permit buying in rail-tankcar-size lots), a machine shop with a four-ton overhead hoist, a paint shop, battery department, gasoline car repair pits, and an electric truck garage with receptacles for charging.

On the vehicle maintenance forms used in the Anheuser-Busch garage, the electric truck driver had these categories for pointing out problems with the battery: burnt strap, burnt lug, burnt jumper, leaky jar, dead cell, burnt jar, battery needs filling, no power, runs slow, or clean jumper lugs. For motors, he could cite: armature burnt out, field coil burnt out, field coil grounded, motor hanger broke, clean commutators, turn commutators, new brushes needed, or new bearings needed.

Nationwide Prohibition took effect via the 18th amendment on January 16, 1920, although some states and localities had voted themselves "dry" before that. A variety of forces worked together to get the amendment passed. One group was the anti-saloon league, which was unhappy that brewers owned taverns or had them tightly bound by contract. Indeed the term "tied house" was used to describe the relationship. (The phrase "lock, stock, and barrel" apparently came from the description of a brewery's hold on its taverns.) As brewers competed, the number of taverns increased and one of the public's criticisms was that there were "too many" taverns.

In any case, the "dries" won the day, and for the next thirteen years, commercial beer deliveries were a thing of the past.

The truck is a 1912 Alco, and what appear to be the words Yonkers Brewery are barely discernible on the sign on the side of the truck bed. *National Automotive History Collection, Detroit Public Library*

The Dobler Brewing Company, in Albany, used this pair of 1912 Peerless trucks, which were built in Cleveland, Ohio. They are shown with a high load of empty barrels. *Smithsonian Institution*

Brewer Jacob Ruppert, of New York City, used this 1912 Hewitt seven-ton truck. Note the roll-down curtains. Hewitts were made in New York City and the firm became part of Mack. *Smithsonian Institution*

A circa-1912 Kissel used by the Chester Brewing Company, of Chester, Pennsylvania. Kissels were built in Hartford, Wisconsin, from 1908 until 1931. *The William F. Harrah Automobile Foundation*

The Cold Springs Brewery used a 1913 Atterbury Model D three-ton truck built in Buffalo. *Smithsonian Institution*

A circa-1913 Dart, used by the brewers of Feigenspan. Dart trucks have been built since 1903, and the firm's current location is Kansas City, Missouri. *Frank Malatesta*

Kleiber trucks were built in San Francisco from 1914 until 1937. The original caption on this picture said: "Photo of Mr. Kleiber & factory crews in Kleiber factory at the completion of a truck for the S. F. Enterprise Brewing Co." Though much of the truck is obscured by the workers, both the brewer's name and the truck make are visible. *American Automobile Manufacturers Assn.*

A 1914 Kleiber carrying beer barrels for the Milwaukee Brewery of San Francisco, California. *Bill West*

An unidentified make of truck carrying barrels of Miller beer in 1914. Note the "Miller Café" sign on the building. Prior to Prohibition, brewers could own taverns. *Miller Brewing Company*

Protiwiner Export, brewed by the Louis Bergdoll Brewing Company, was carried in this circa-1914 White. *American Truck Historical Society*

A circa-1914 Palmer-Moore truck (built in Syracuse) carries cases of Congress beer. The Palmer-Moore came in one-ton and two-ton models with four-cylinder engines. *Chuck Rhoads*

A 1914 White owned by the C. Schmidt & Sons Brewing Company of Philadelphia, Pennsylvania. According to Charles Wacker, the movable stakes in the rear were sealed with hot linseed oil to prevent splinters. Also, if they were painted, the paint wouldn't last long because the stakes were continually being lifted in and out. *Charles Wacker*

Garden City Brewery in Chicago, Illinois, makers of Primator beer, used this 1914 White. Note the fancy striping and lettering, as well as the chain drive. *American Truck Historical Society*

A mid-teens White, used in St. Louis, Missouri, by Gast Brewery, brewers of Alpen Brau. The folded tarp is stored on the cab roof. *American Truck Historical Society*

Dorris trucks were built in St. Louis and this one—from before World War I—was used by the Gast Brewery. The small sign says: "Capacity 11 bbls or 75 cases." *Chuck Rhoads*

Stroh's beer is carried in a Horner truck, circa 1917. Horner trucks were built in Wyandotte, Michigan, and only for a few years. They came in five models with a one- to five-ton capacity, chain drive, and claimed a horsepower range of 33 to 46 horsepower. *Chuck Rhoads*

A circa-1915 Pierce-Arrow operated by the Peter Hand Brewery in Chicago, with a load of Meister Brau. Pierce-Arrow trucks were built in Buffalo by a firm much better known for its high-quality automobiles. *University of Michigan*

This mid-teens Schacht is shown with a load of Happy Days beer, brewed by the Crown Brewing Company. Schacht trucks were built in Cincinnati, Ohio, in one-ton, two-ton and three-ton models using worm drive. *Chuck Rhoads*

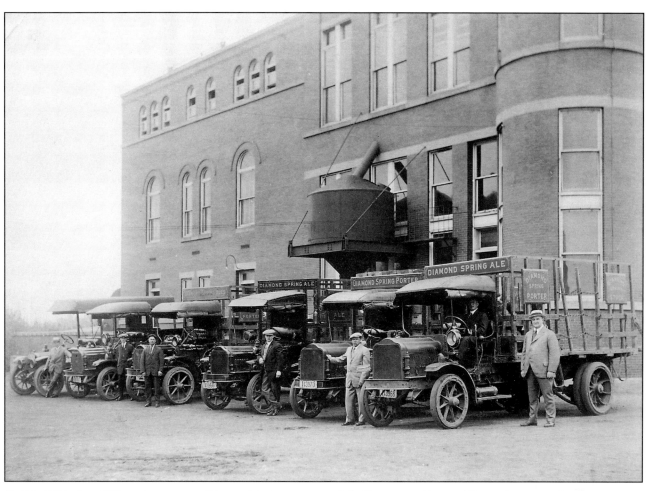

Six World War I-era Whites used to carry Diamond Springs porter and ale. There was a Diamond Springs brewery in Lawrence, Massachusetts. *American Truck Historical Society*

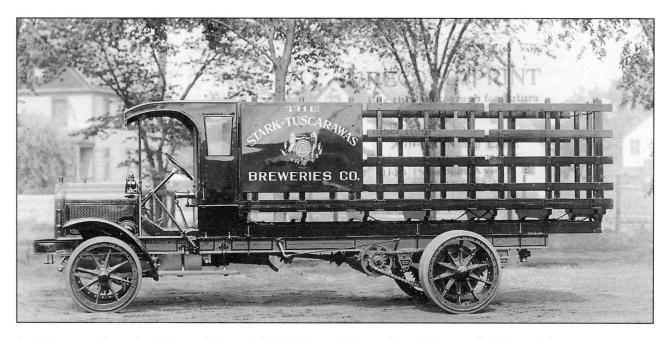

Stark-Tuscarawas Breweries in Canton, Ohio, used this 1915 five-ton White stake truck. *American Truck Historical Society*

Barrels of Peipp's Hollander beer in a Chicago distributor's 1916 White. *American Truck Historical Society*

The Wacker & Birk Brewing Company, makers of Perfecto beer, used this pair of 1916 Whites to carry empty barrels. A ramp for rolling the barrels is in an upright position in the center of the load on the truck in the foreground. *American Truck Historical Society*

A World War I-vintage truck carrying a display of Budweiser cases in a parade. *Anheuser-Busch Archives*

A Schlitz distributor in Chicago used this circa-1917 Diamond-T. It's shown carrying beer cases. Diamond-Ts were produced in Chicago from 1911 until 1966. *Chuck Rhoads*

Wm. Hartig Fine Beers, of Watertown, Wisconsin, used this three-ton 1917 FWD built by the Four Wheel Drive Auto Company. FWDs were, and still are, built in Clintonville, Wisconsin. *Chuck Rhoads*

The name of the brewery appears to be Kips Bay Brewing Company, with an address of 662 First Avenue, New York, New York. The truck is an early Mack Bulldog. *Mack Museum*

A World War I-vintage Sterling, built in Milwaukee, Wisconsin, carrying Pabst Blue Ribbon. Initially, Sterling trucks had been called Sternbergs, but the name was changed due to anti-German sentiment during World War I. Some histories of Prohibition suggest that the amendment passed in part because of this sentiment, since Germans and German-Americans were associated with beer. *Chuck Rhoads*

A circa-1917 Pierce-Arrow carries Maltosia, brewed by the German-American Brewing Company. *University of Michigan*

RIGHT: This picture shows a 1917 truck show held in New York City. A number of trucks are shown outfitted for carrying beer. To the left of center is a Packard display including a truck loaded with barrels. To the right is the Mack display and on the far side of the truck with barrels is a stake truck with the lettering "Wm. Peters Brewing Co." on the side. Two other trucks with barrels are in the background. *American Automobile Manufacturers Assn.*

Two late-teens Morelands picking up beer at a San Diego wholesaler of Maier beer. The holes in the truck tires are to give a more cushioned ride. The truck in the rear has solid tires and right-hand steering. *Bill West*

This was a promotional vehicle built for use by Anheuser-Busch. A number of photos exist of it appearing in various public relations roles. Whether it was a single vehicle, or one of several, is unknown. *The William F. Harrah Automobile Foundation*

A circa-1918 Pierce-Arrow carries beer barrels. Note the dock bumper between the cab and the bed. It might also have been used to cushion barrels and kegs during unloading. *University of Michigan*

A World War I-vintage GMC used in Detroit to carry Detroit-Bohemian beer. *GMC*

Chapter Three

Prohibition Rules the Decade
1921–1930

The 1920s were an important period in the development of trucks and trucking. Just prior to 1919, World War I had ended, and the truck had demonstrated its advantages over the horse for wartime uses. In most commercial fields, trucks were being substituted for horses.

However, due to Prohibition (1920–1933), supposedly no beer was distributed or sold. Surviving breweries turned to soft drinks, yeast, malt, and other products. Some breweries made "near-beer," which could contain up to one-half of one percent of alcohol, though there seem to be very few photos of trucks of the Prohibition era that appeared to be distributing "near-beers."

Old truck fans enjoy watching TV reruns of *The Untouchables*, because almost every episode has a few trucks making illegal deliveries. However, nearly all of them purportedly carried bootleg whiskey, which was a higher-priced and more profitable cargo to carry. No doubt there was bootleg beer as well, but pictures of it being hauled in trucks are difficult to come by.

Selling beer was illegal, but selling beer-making supplies was not—Anheuser-Busch sold Budweiser Barley Malt Syrup, ostensibly for cooking and baking, but really used for home brewing. During Prohibition, many individuals continued to make beer in their bathtubs—an earlier wave of "microbreweries." Product quality varied.

During Prohibition, Anheuser-Busch devoted some of its idle wagon-building capacity toward the building of truck bodies. One was a refrigerated body that relied on brine for cooling. It was referred to as the A. B. C. body, with the letters standing for "Automatic Brine Circulation," and was sold to dairies and meat packers. A company publication stated, "By the use of 150 pounds of ice in this body, and 30 pounds of salt, an inside temperature of three to ten degrees above zero can be maintained for a period of 24 hours. The motion of the truck in transit circulates the zero brine to produce the low temperature inside the truck body."

Bevo was a near-beer, legal during Prohibition. This Ford Model T, which probably dates from about 1915, was used during Prohibition in Chattanooga, Tennessee. *Anheuser-Busch Archives*

Toward the end of Prohibition, Anheuser-Busch redirected this operation to the construction of electrical refrigeration units for stationary installations.

The second well-known body that Anheuser-Busch shops built was the Lamsteed Kampkar, a camping body that fit on a Ford Model T chassis. The sides of the body folded downward into a horizontal position and became beds on each side of the car. While initial interest was great, it tapered off, and apparently production ceased in the mid-1920s. The Kampkar bodies could fit other chassis; a 1921 issue of a company magazine pictures a Kampkar body on a White. The Anheuser-Busch body shop also built station wagon bodies and bus bodies.

By 1933, the truck had developed to a point just shy of being "modern." The paved highway system had been expanded and the trucks' pneumatic tires allowed them to make deliveries outside of urban areas.

An early-1920s Packard used to distribute Bevo near-beer in Oklahoma City. At the rear of the truck sits a figure of a fox, possibly the brew's emblem. Packard trucks were built in Detroit from 1905 until 1923, although the firm continued building autos until well after World War II. *McCabe-Powers Body Company*

A Budweiser distributor in Arizona restored this mid-1920s Ford.

A restored Ford Model TT stake body truck, used by a Miller's distributor for promotional purposes. *Miller Brewing Company*

Anheuser-Busch Horse Vans

When writing about beer trucks and thinking of the industry, one cannot avoid some of the very fancy trucks for carrying horses associated with the Anheuser-Busch family and firm. They include some fancy vans August Busch had for his riding horses, as well as vans for carrying the company's well-known teams of Clydesdales.

August Busch used this horse van, mounted on a late 1920s GMC chassis, for fox hunting. On the roof of the cab are figures of two foxes. *Anheuser-Busch Archives*

An extremely fancy horse van on a late 1920s bus chassis used by August Busch, Sr. *Anheuser-Busch Archives*

Anheuser-Busch has long had huge Clydesdale horses, which they used for promotional purposes. This mid-1950s GMC tractor pulled the trailer that carried the horses from appearance to appearance. *Anheuser-Busch Archives*

This mid-1920s Ford was used by a wholesaler for bottlers' supplies, including malt and hops, useful to those who did their brewing at home. *Lorin Sorensen*

The Pennsylvania Brewing Company was founded in Pittsburgh in 1986 and is a microbrewery—one of many small "boutique" brewers that are sprouting up everywhere. This is a restored 1926 Graham Brothers truck that the brewery currently uses to promote Penn Pilsner, one of their brews. Graham Brothers trucks were closely related to Dodges. *Penn Brewery*

Breweries elsewhere in the world continued their operations, oblivious to Prohibition in the United States. This mid-1920s Scammell, a British-built truck, was used by Guinness in Ireland. *Guinness Archives*

During Prohibition, Anheuser-Busch sold yeast, and other products, in order to stay in business. Driver-salesmen delivered the yeast in small quantities to retail stores. The motto "We Rise to Every Occasion" is painted on the side of the cargo compartment. The truck is a 1929 Chevrolet. *Anheuser-Busch Archives*

U.S. trucks were both exported and assembled overseas. This Ford Model AA, circa 1930, with right-hand steering, was used by Guinness in Ireland. *Guinness Archives*

This neon Pabst sign was probably put up after Prohibition ended. The sign was installed by Everbrite Electric Signs, of South Milwaukee, Wisconsin. It's being delivered in a Ford Model A closed-cab pickup. *Everbrite*

Chapter Four

Happy Days Are Here Again
1931–1940

This was an important decade for the beer industry, with Prohibition ending in 1933. As stated in *The History of Beer in California*, "It was the single busiest day in California beer distribution history, and the state celebrated in the shimmering style for which it was already famous. In Los Angeles, actress Jean Harlow 'christened' a beer delivery truck. Mae West was also on hand to help celebrate as the beer trucks left the warehouse. . . . In Northern California at one minute after midnight on April 7, distributors began leaving local breweries for deliveries to San Francisco hotels. A delivery truck equipped with red police lights and a siren delivered kegs of beer to the Mark Hopkins [hotel] which had temporarily transformed its dining room into a beer garden."

This White has 1931 plates so it may be loading "near-beer." The picture was taken in Chicago and the sign on the building touts Atlas Special Brew. *American Truck Historical Society*

South Side Brewing Company of Chicago used this early 1930s White. Note that the workers handling beer wore heavy aprons. The firm's products were called Ambrosia and Nectar. There was an Ambrosia Brewing Company in Chicago. *American Truck Historical Society*

Federal and state laws were changed to allow breweries back into business. Most states established stricter regulations on the distribution system for beer, setting up distributors who stood between the brewers and the taverns and retail outlets. Beer trucks pictured in earlier chapters usually belonged to the brewers, while trucks pictured from this point forward generally belong to distributors.

Distribution Developments

Each state established its own rules for distributing beer. Some states would sell beer and other alcoholic beverages only in state-run retail stores. Most states did allow retail sales through stores, clubs, and taverns. However, a "distributor" system stood between these retail outlets and the breweries. The new system was to overcome some pre-Prohibition problems of brewery control over retailers, especially taverns. The new system was also supposed to improve governments' ability to collect taxes on beer. Some states had "at rest" requirements, which meant that all beer had to stop and be "at rest" in a distributor's warehouse before being delivered to retail outlets. Some states gave distributors

A 1932–1933 Chevrolet sedan delivery used by Anheuser-Busch to distribute yeast and Budweiser Barley Malt Syrup. Malt syrup was used to facilitate home brewing and sold very well during Prohibition. (August Busch, Jr., would later note that the company "ended up the biggest bootlegging supply house in the United States.") It continued to sell well for a few years after Prohibition ended. *Anheuser-Busch Archives*

This early-1930s Dodge panel has Schlitz markings. *Eight-Point Trailer Corp., Los Angeles*

"exclusive" territories, thereby restricting competition. (Over the years, beer distributorships have proved to be quite lucrative and distributors fight off attempts to modify the system. The most recent attacks have been from large mass merchandisers who prefer to bypass intermediaries.)

After Prohibition ended, beer was packaged and distributed in two forms, barrels and 12-ounce returnable bottles. The bottles were carried in wooden cases holding 24. Both the barrels and bottles were reused

and the driver, or driver/salesman, delivering new product would also pick up the empty barrels and cases of empty bottles. In terms of cubic capacity, his truck was always "full." One Los Angeles firm began home deliveries of bottled beer, modeling their service after that offered by dairies. In 1935, the California state government banned home delivery of beer.

The need for refrigeration following delivery also influenced distribution patterns. Southland Corporation, the parent company of 7-Eleven convenience stores, was originally an ice distributor and began carrying beer in its ice outlets, since they also possessed the ability to keep it cool. As larger grocery stores were built, some by chains, they also had mechanical cooling devices for refrigerating some products, including beer.

Drivers who doubled as salesmen made deliveries, following established routes. Each morning they would load their truck with what they thought they could sell. They would then stop at each customer where they would remove cases of empty bottles, and empty kegs. They would make a sales pitch and encourage the retailer or bar owner to put up a few signs or displays in addition to buying more beer. The sale would be completed, and the driver/salesman would then unload a portion of his truck and fill out a sales invoice—and then drive on to the next stop. Driver/salesmen were paid on a salary plus

A 1932 Dodge truck used by Stroh's. The tarp protected against both rain and sun. *Stroh Brewery Company*

The big day! The original caption on this photo said: "Trucks at Gluecks Brewery waiting to pull out when Prohibition ends." The truck in the foreground is a LaFrance Republic, built in Alma, Michigan. *Minnesota Historical Society; reproduced with permission.*

During Prohibition, the F.X. Matt Brewing Company of Utica survived by bottling and selling soft drinks, fruit beverages, malt tonics, syrups, extracts, and distilled water. When Prohibition ended they went back to making beer. This is the delivery fleet they had available at Prohibition's end to distribute Utica Club Pilsener. *The Matt Brewing Company*

commission basis—they had an incentive to sell more product and to keep customers happy.

A 1933 report entitled *The Brewing Industry* gave these estimates of beer and its distribution costs: Beer in barrels cost $3.75 to manufacture; $1.00 to deliver; $.25 for sales and collections; $.30 for advertising; and $.25 for barrel upkeep and replacement—totaling $5.55 per barrel. For bottled beer (with bottles and cases returned) the manufacturing costs per barrel were the same, but bottling and delivery cost $3.30 per barrel, plus $.50 for sales and collections, and $.45 for advertising, totaling $8.00 per barrel. If there were no returns of cases or bottles, the costs of bottled beer per barrel would more than double. Hence, the economies of that era forced the driver to pick up empties.

New Era for Trucks

The trucks used by the industry to distribute beer were much improved over those in use when Prohibition began. They now rode on pneumatic tires, had four-wheel brakes, could travel at higher speeds, came with enclosed cabs, and were styled with a slight hint of streamlining. Many would be insulated, and a few would even have mechanical refrigeration. By the decade's end, some very streamlined beer delivery trucks were produced, especially in Canada; this streamlining effort was never matched again.

The newly vitalized Anheuser-Busch was at the forefront of truck and body development. A company house organ, *A-B Ink*, reported: "Prohibition ended in 1933 and Anheuser-Busch realized how greatly truck hauling had developed during the thirteen "dry" years. . . . The facilities of the Bottling Plant, designed for rail-

road cars, were adapted for truck loading and unloading and office procedures for truck shipments were established. . . . Our research department started to devote time and study to the proper icing of trucks, adequate protection against heat and cold and improved routines for loading and unloading. . . ." In 1938, the firm began a uniform truck-painting program. Wholesalers were urged to paint their trucks in a red and green scheme and carry the slogan: "Anheuser-Busch / BUDWEISER / everywhere." Stencils were provided.

Using trucks for advertising and promotion went well beyond stenciled signage, however. While streamlining autos was taken for granted, several truckmakers adapted streamlining techniques to their products as well. Diamond-T built stylish trucks with limousine-like qualities (sharing the front fender-mounted parking lights with the 1938 Buick, for example). Dodge trucks had their own "airflow" version that was used mainly for petroleum-product tankers. White retained Count Sakhnoffsky, a noted industrial designer. Since a completed truck required the inputs of both the truck builder and the truck body builder, a collaborative effort was needed to ensure that the streamlined truck's "lines" blended with the body's lines as well. Fruehauf and Heil were two body builders who turned out streamlined trailers and bodies during this decade.

RIGHT: Consumer's Brewing Company, of Warwick, Rhode Island, used this early-1930s White flatbed to carry both barrels and cases. The firm brewed Consumers Ale. *American Truck Historical Society*

This 1932 REO panel truck was used by the advertising department of Kings Brewery, in Brooklyn, New York. It would carry posters and stand-up displays for merchants and bar owners to use for promoting Kings beer. Often the merchant or bar owner would be given a free case or two in appreciation of his using the display. REOs were built in Lansing, and the letters stand for Ransome E. Olds. *American Truck Historical Society*

A 1933 Chevrolet with a display of Schlitz beer. *Eight-Point Trailer Corp., Los Angeles*

Three 1933 Diamond-T trucks, carrying Schlitz beer. *Smithsonian Institution*

The make of this truck is unknown: it's possibly a Sterling. Lettering on the side of the hood says: "Cummins Diesel Power." This was one of the earliest diesel-powered trucks. The auto is a 1935 Auburn, also diesel-powered. Diesels came into use later in the 1930s and were widely used during and after World War II. The truck carries Lucky Lager, brewed in San Francisco. *Watson & Meehan, San Francisco*

A 1933–1934 Ford stake truck used to haul Green Seal beer. The Ford salesman's coupe, of similar vintage, is on the left; it also has "Green Seal" markings. *Lorin Sorensen*

ABC beer was distributed in Fresno, using this 1933 GMC with an Eight-Point body. *Eight-Point Trailer Corp., Los Angeles*

Two views of an enclosed Heil body on an early 1930s International used for carrying cases of Gettelman beer, brewed in Milwaukee. Inside each side compartment are racks that are two cases wide and three cases high. The Heil Company is a well-known truck body-builder that still exists in the Milwaukee area. *The Heil Co.*

This 1933 International pickup was by a beer distributor. Having no beer brand name showing is unusual; usually the brewer would supply decals. Small trucks were used by salesmen who would take advance orders and distribute point-of-sale promotional materials. *Navistar Archives*

An early-1930s Mack, used to carry New York's Lion beer and ale. *American Truck Historical Society*

The most challenging truck and trailer streamlining project originated in Canada, where beer advertising efforts were severely limited. As a way around this limitation, some Canadian brewers (Labatt claims to be first) decided to have designed and built a fleet of beer delivery trucks so unique and so attractive that they served as rolling advertisements.

Practical considerations still ruled the day, however. Keeping beer cool was a challenge, and the needs varied by geography, climate, and the length of time that the beer would be exposed. Most beer bodies are enclosed for security and weather protection, including a top that will reflect the sunlight. Some bodies were insulated, and ice could be used to keep them cool. Eventually, mechanical refrigeration units were installed in some markets. In markets where open trucks were used, a light-colored tarpaulin, either wet or dry, would be thrown over the load in hot weather.

A 1933 trade journal described a body built by the Batavia Body Company:

It is fully enclosed with side and double-rear doors. Its capacity is 88 cases of beer. An aisle 28 inches wide is provided from the side-door opening. Rings, chain and snaps are provided to prevent cases from falling into the aisle. The interior is slatted with 3/8-inch by 3-inch slats spaced on 8-inch centers. There is an Eberhard folding step for each entrance. The beer case dimensions were: length, 19 1/4-inch; width, 12-inch; height, 10 1/4-inch. The body loading space dimensions are: length, 122 inches; width, 63 inches; height 62 inches. . . .

For beer in kegs, Brockway has designed a brewers' body that is a heavy-duty flareboard express with solid headboard and high stakes at rear. It is designed to properly load 40, 60, 80 or 100 kegs (half-barrels) depending upon the size of chassis. A single half-barrel (full) weighs 195 pounds. It is 24 inches long and 19 inches in diameter.

An article in a 1937 trade magazine, *Power Wagon*, described a low-bed truck body used around ports. The bed was low enough that, when parked next to a sidewalk, it allowed one man to handle heavy loads:

Among the users in San Francisco operating these GMC low bed trucks is the General Brewing Company and Rainier, the low bed permitting one man to unload kegs of beer onto the sidewalk without the use of the usual pad which is placed on the sidewalk to receive the keg when rolled off the truck with the usual height of the bed.

The General Brewing trucks are painted pure white with the trade name Lucky Lager painted in very large letters on both sides and in smaller letters on the doors of the cab. Stakes on both sides of the truck and at the rear permit loading and unloading from three points. Over the cab is a neon sign reading "LUCKY LAGER" which is operated from the truck battery.

In 1940, the nation's 10 largest brewers, in descending order of popularity, were Anheuser-Busch, Pabst, Schlitz, Schaefer, Ballantine, Ruppert, Falstaff, Liebmann, Hamm's, and Blatz. The top 10 controlled 24 percent of the market. The top 10 beer-producing states, in descending order, were New York, Pennsylvania, Wisconsin, Missouri, Illinois, Ohio, New Jersey, Michigan, Minnesota, and California. The major beer-consuming states, in descending order, were New York, Pennsylvania, Illinois, Ohio, Michigan, New Jersey, California, Wisconsin, Massachusetts, and Minnesota. In this particular year, New York and Pennsylvania consumed just over one-quarter of all beer brewed in the United States. At this time, just over 50 percent of all beer was distributed through wholesalers, 32 percent directly to retailers, and 17 percent through the brewers' own sales branches.

Feigenspan beer was brewed in Newark, New Jersey, and carried in this early-1930s Mack. *American Truck Historical Society*

Old Shay ale and Steinhaus beer carried in an early-1930s Mack with dual rear axles. At the far right of the sign on the truck's side are the words: "100% Union Made," a meaningful slogan in the 1930s. *American Truck Historical Society*

An early-1930s Mack tractor with a semitrailer used by a Seitz beer distributor in Easton, Pennsylvania. Trailers and semitrailers were introduced into the trucking industry during the 1920s. Tractors with semitrailers were used for many beer deliveries in urban areas. They actually have a shorter turning radius than straight trucks of similar capacity. *Charles Wacker*

Labatt's Beer Trucks

The best-known beer trucks are the Labatt's trucks of the late 1930s. In Canada, beer advertising was strictly controlled and Labatt's management believed that distinctive trucks would call attention to their product. Count Alexis de Sakhnoffsky, who was retained by Labatt in 1935 through the White Company, designed the rigs. White supplied the tractor chassis; Fruehauf, the trailer; and the Smith Brothers of Toronto did the bodywork. At least 25 trucks, consisting of four different models, were produced and were on Canadian roads from the late 1930s well into the 1950s. They were produced both before and after World War II.

A straight frame truck, probably a White, with streamlined Labatt's features. *Volvo/White*

Two custom-designed White tractors linked with Fruehauf trailers used to promote and carry Labatt's beer. Note the forward slant of the windshields. *Volvo/White*

A rear view of the Fruehauf-built semitrailer. Note the fender skirts and fancy door hardware. *Fruehauf*

A 1948 White COE tractor substituted for the original, pulling a prewar custom Labatt's semitrailer. *American Truck Historical Society*

This 1933 Studebaker was operated by Rubsam & Horrmann Brewing Company, of Staten Island. Note the radiator guard. *American Truck Historical Society*

An early-1930s White used by a New York City distributor of Ebling's Extra beer. The white sidewalls are unusual. Note that the windshield opens at the bottom to increase air circulation through the cab. *American Truck Historical Society*

This White has 1933 Ohio plates and was used by the Cleveland Home Brewing Company, brewers of Clevelander beer. *American Truck Historical Society*

Dominion Brewery of Toronto, Canada, ran this early-1930s White with an insulated Fruehauf semitrailer. *American Truck Historical Society*

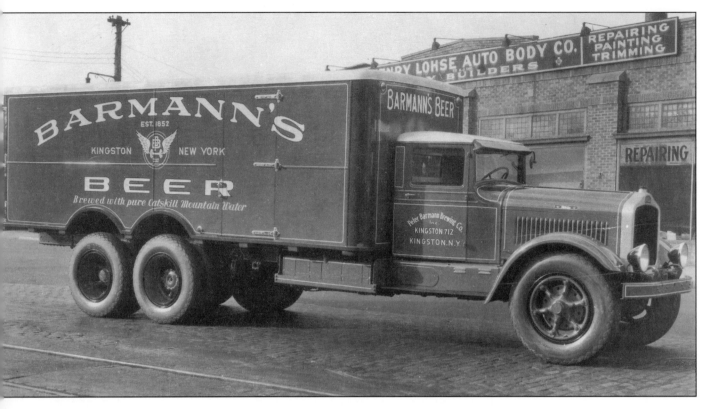

Barmann's beer was carried in this early-1930s White with twin rear axles. The brewery was located in Kingston, New York. *American Truck Historical Society*

Tying down a load of new barrels on an early-1930s White flatbed, operated by Pickwick Ale. The barrels seem uniformly new and "Haffenreffer & Co. Boston," the name of either the brewer or cooper, is stenciled on top of each. *American Truck Historical Society*

Jacob Hornung Brewing Company, of Philadelphia, brewer of Hornung's White Bock, used this early-1930s White flatbed. Note the tarp on top apparently has "cut-outs" for running lights. *American Truck Historical Society*

A fleet of four Whites from the early 1930s used by the Schultz Brewing Company of Union City, New Jersey. *American Truck Historical Society*

Three 1934 Chevrolet sedan deliveries being delivered to Anheuser-Busch, where they will be used by salesmen for the firm's yeast and malt syrup products. The truck tractor is a 1933 Ford. *Automobile Transport, Inc.*

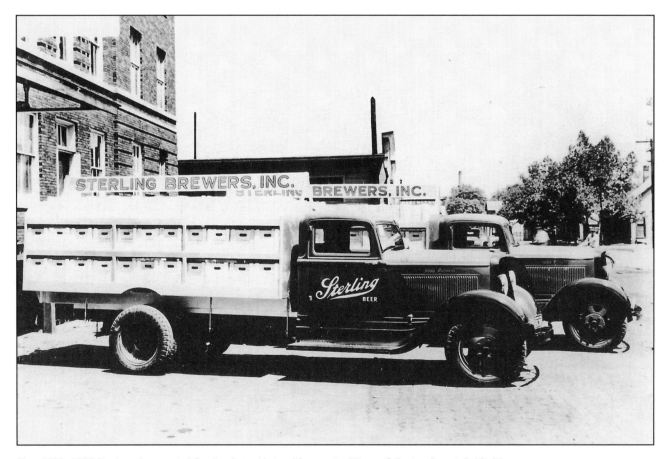

Two 1933–1935 Dodges that carried Sterling beer. *National Automotive History Collection, Detroit Public Library*

The nameplate on the side of the hood was changed from "Dodge" to read "Grain Belt," the beer brewed by the Minneapolis Brewing Company. *National Automotive History Collection, Detroit Public Library*

Blatz Old Heidelberg was distributed in this 1934 GMC. *McCabe-Powers Body Company*

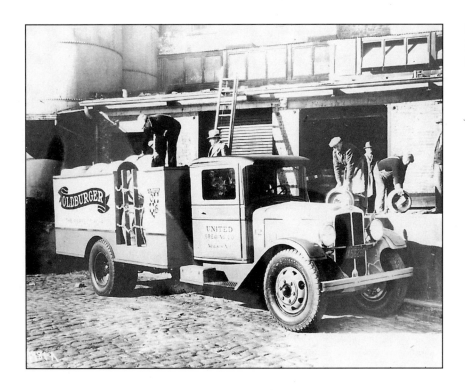

United Brewing Company, in Newark, New Jersey, used this 1934 Indiana for handling its Oldburger beer. *Volvo/White*

A mid-1930s International stake truck used by a Carling distributor. Other signs on the truck list O'Keefe's and Amos brews. *Navistar Archives*

An early-1930s Indiana being loaded with cases of Augustiner Brew. Letters on the side of the cases say "Columbus, O." (presumably Columbus, Ohio). Indiana trucks were built first in Marion, Ohio, then Cleveland. *American Truck Historical Society*

Golden Age beer being hauled by a Spokane, Washington, distributor. The tractor is an early-1930s International with a sleeper cab. *Navistar Archives*

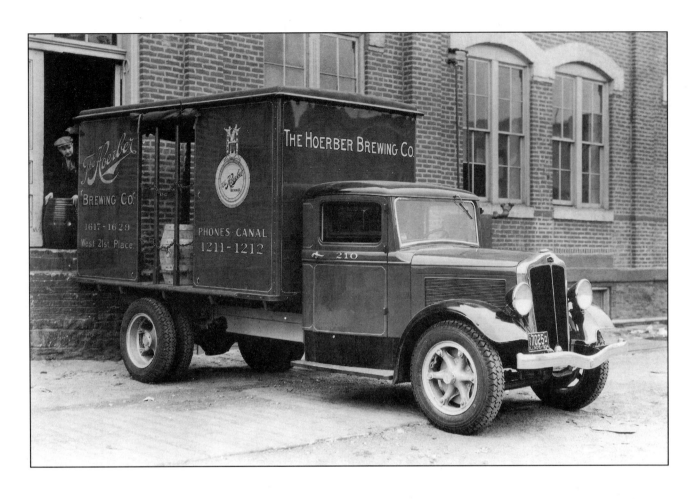

Hoerber beer was distributed in this 1934 White that has Illinois license plates. The worker at the rear is loading kegs. *American Truck Historical Society*

An early-1930s Mack Bulldog carrying barrels of Tally-Ho beer. *George Humphrey*

Aetna ale and lager were distributed on these 1934 Whites in Hartford, Connecticut. *American Truck Historical Society*

A 1934–1935 White carrying barrels of Renners Old Oxford Ale, brewed in Youngstown, Ohio. In front of the rear wheel is a braided "keg bumper," used to cushion the fall of the keg, and to keep it from rolling. *American Truck Historical Society*

Greenway Brewing Company in Syracuse, brewers of Greenway's India Pale Ale, used this pair of 1934 Whites. *American Truck Historical Society*

Resch's Pilsener on a 1934 White. The truck has right-hand drive, so the photo was probably taken outside the United States. *American Truck Historical Society*

This 1934 White was used to distribute SK Lager Beer in St. Louis. The Schorr-Kolkschneider Brewing Company brewed the beer. *American Truck Historical Society*

A mid-1930s White operated by Globe Brewery of Baltimore. The arrow on top contains a sign saying, "It hits the spot." The sign along the side reads: "Good in '17 . . . Better Today!"—a reference to Prohibition. *National Automotive History Collection, Detroit Public Library*

Golden Brew beer, brewed in Harrison, New Jersey, was distributed in this 1934–1935 White. *American Truck Historical Society*

Workers unloading barrels of Krueger's beer from a 1934 White. Photo was taken in Newark, New Jersey. *Volvo/White*

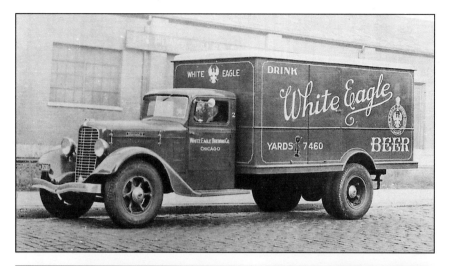

A mid-1930s Diamond-T two-ton Model 351 carrying White Eagle beer, apparently brewed in Chicago. The truck could hold 25 barrels or 50 half-barrels. *Smithsonian Institution*

A 1935 Diamond-T one-ton Model 211 carrying Birk's beer. *American Trucking Associations*

A mid-1930s Fageol with a load of Edel-brau. Note the streamlining of the enclosed box. The markings on truck are confusing: The top lines say "Sunset Motor Freight," the middle line talks about the beer, and the bottom line says "Ellensburg Brewing Co." While it's possible that the truck was used to haul both general freight and beer, this would have been unusual because of the post-Prohibition laws regarding beer distribution and the 1935 Motor Carrier Act. *Bill West*

A 1935 Federal owned by the Miller Brewing Company of Milwaukee, carrying empty barrels. Federal trucks were built in Detroit until shortly after World War II. *American Automobile Manufacturers Assn.*

A mid-1930s International outfitted to haul Acme Non-Fattening Beer in Astoria, Oregon. *New Haven Carriage & Auto Works, Portland, Oregon*

This fancy 1935 Stewart carried C & L Edelbrau. Stewart trucks were built in Buffalo during the period from 1912 to 1941. *American Automobile Manufacturers Assn.*

The Boston Ginger Ale distributor also handled Schlitz beer, Wehle Mulehead ale, and King's beer and ale. The truck is a 1935 White. The distributor's Boston Health Permit number is painted on the side of the cowl. *American Truck Historical Society*

Keeley Brewing Company, in Chicago, used this 1935 White, shown being loaded with barrels. In front of the worker standing on the street is a "keg bumper." *American Truck Historical Society*

National Breweries, Ltd., (probably in Canada) used this 1934 White to carry Dow Old Stock Ale. *American Truck Historical Society*

A Kranz stake body was placed on this 1935 White for an East St. Louis, Illinois, distributor of Central beer. *Kranz Automotive Body Company*

A 1936–1937 Diamond-T, with a General body, used by a Chicago distributor of Schlitz. During this era, Diamond-T trucks were probably the most stylish trucks produced, but relatively few pictures were found showing them as beer trucks. *General Body Company, Chicago*

In Philadelphia, Ortliebs was delivered to tap rooms in this 1936 International with a Wacker body. Charles Wacker recalled that the owner of this brewery insisted that a tarp always cover the load to protect it from the sun. *Charles Wacker*

A circa-1936 Kenworth pulling two Reliance trailers, one a semi, the other, full. The product hauled is Rainier beer. *Reliance*

A mid-1930s Sterling, carrying a load of Golden Glow beer and ale, brewed in northern California. *American Truck Historical Society*

Drewry's Ale and Lager beer were carried by a South Bend, Indiana, distributor in a 1936 Studebaker COE. *Antique Studebaker Club*

Burke's Ale was distributed in Long Island City, New York, in this 1936 White. *American Truck Historical Society*

A 1936 Studebaker that carried Hohenadel beer in Philadelphia. Truck body builder Charles Wacker said that the body was low because the interior of the brewery had low ceilings. *Charles Wacker*

The Dallas Brewery used this 1936 White to haul White Rose beer. The rack in the top of the box is for empty cases. Load-bearing roofs had to be specified and they cost more. They usually came with a railing and a ladder to reach them. Most enclosed bodies could also be completely locked. *American Truck Historical Society*

A 1937 Diamond-T loaded with cases of Schlitz. Open display of beer in this manner is unusual. *Mike Pagel*

A 1937–1938 Dodge, with an Eight-Point beer body, used for distributing Schlitz. *Eight-Point Trailer Corp., Los Angeles*

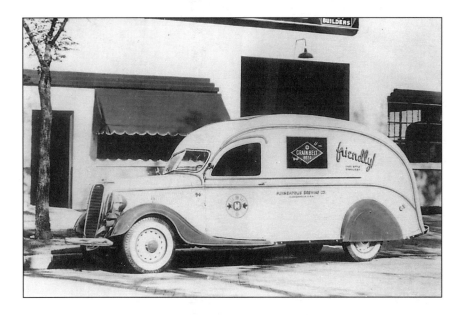

A 1937 Ford with a streamlined body, used for delivering Grain Belt beer. *Lorin Sorensen*

Streamlining was popular in the 1930s. General Body Company created this proposal for a streamlined Schlitz beer body. *General Body Company, Chicago*

A late-1930s GMC with a streamlined body used to promote and carry O'Keefe's in Canada. *W. A. Drew*

Stroh's beer was carried in this 1937 GMC tractor-semitrailer combination. *American Truck Historical Society*

Lucky Lager was carried in this 1937 GMC cab-over. *Columbia Body & Equipment Company*

Doane trucks were built in San Francisco. They had low beds and were used to dray cargo around ports. They're often pictured in West Coast ports carrying newsprint rolls or bags of coffee. The Doane factory built a low-bed body on this 1937 GMC for carrying Rainier beer. *Bill West*

A Duquesne distributor in Elkins, West Virginia, used this 1937 International. The body was built by Schnabel. Duquesne beer was brewed in Pittsburgh. *Historical Society of Western Pennsylvania*

A Duquesne distributor in Canonsburg, Pennsylvania, used this 1937 Studebaker. The Schnabel-built body is for barrels and kegs. *Historical Society of Western Pennsylvania*

In Bridgeport, New York, this 1937 White was used for handling Beverwyck beer and ale. *American Truck Historical Society*

An attractive stake body used for distributing Black Horse ale and porter. The truck is a circa-1937 White. The doors on the side of the truck body open to allow for unloading while the truck is parallel to the sidewalk. *American Truck Historical Society*

This 1937 White with a streamlined Labatt's trailer was displayed at the 1937 Great Lakes Exposition. Later, a more streamlined tractor-semitrailer would appear (see related sidebar). *National Automotive History Collection, Detroit Public Library*

Sunrise beer and ale moved in this late-1930s White. The mascot on the side of the truck is named "Sunny Rise." *American Truck Historical Society*

A 1937 Chevrolet that carried Ballantine's for a Newark distributor. Ballantine's was brewed in Newark, New Jersey. The body was built by Peter Wendel & Sons. *A. L. Hansen Mfg. Company*

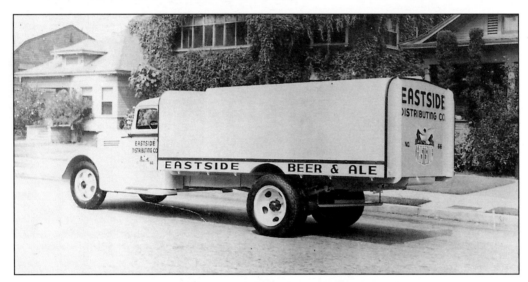

An open body on a 1938 Federal chassis. *Eight-Point Trailer Corp., Los Angeles*

An ultrastreamlined tractor-trailer used to carry Brading's, a Canadian brew. The trailer is by Fruehauf. *Fruehauf*

A late-1930s International panel used by Labatt's in Canada, probably to carry advertising and promotional materials. *Navistar Archives*

Taylor & Bate was a Canadian brewer. This is a streamlined trailer pulled by a late-1930s International tractor. *Navistar Archives*

A Carling's distributor in Detroit used this 1938 Model 805 T White with rear fender skirts and a streamlined trailer. *Volvo/White*

Grain Belt beer was carried in a streamlined refrigerated body on a 1938 White chassis. Note the swept design of the front fender, several years before such a design was used with most autos. *American Truck Historical Society*

Manhattan beer was carried in this 1939 Autocar cab-over, with an insulated body built by J. Metzler & Sons. The truck has Illinois plates. *A. L. Hansen Mfg. Company*

A 1939 Ford COE, with a Heiser body, used to carry Rainier beer. Heiser bodies are built in Seattle. *Geo. Heiser Body Company*

In the foreground is a 1939 Ford, and behind it is a 1937 Chevrolet. Both carry JAX beer. The American Body & Equipment Co., of Dallas, Texas, which has been in business since 1918, built the bodies. *American Body & Equipment Company*

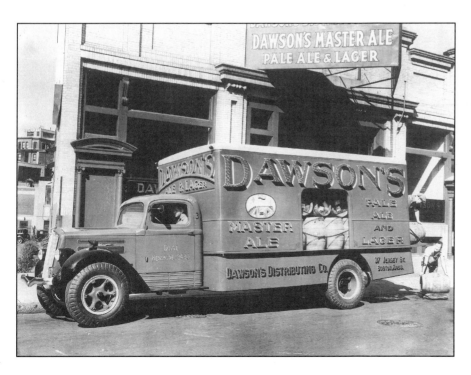

Barrels of Dawson's ale and lager are shown being loaded on this 1939 White in Boston. A keg bumper is barely visible, below the barrel that is on the street. There was a Dawson brewery in New Bedford, Massachusetts. *American Truck Historical Society*

The Hemrich Brewing Company in Seattle ran this late-1930s White with a semitrailer. On its side are advertised the sizes of bottles in which their beer is sold: the 12-ounce "Stubby," the 32-ounce "Jumbo," and the 64-ounce "double Jumbo." *American Truck Historical Society*

The Ohio plates on this White are from 1939. The Wooden Shoe Brewing Company was located in Minister, Ohio. The trailer was built by Fruehauf. *American Truck Historical Society*

Peter Wendel & Sons, Inc., built the refrigerated body for a Feigenspan distributor. Hinges on the rear doors allowed them to open completely and rest against the sides of the body. The truck is a 1940 Chevrolet. *A. L. Hansen Mfg. Company*

Four trucks in front of a Coors distributor, circa 1940. Fords are on each end, Chevrolets in the center. *Adolph Coors Company*

A 1940 Mack cab-over, used by a Pabst distributor. *Mack Museum*

New Life Pilsener was brewed by Goenner & Company, of Johnstown, Pennsylvania, which used this 1940 White with a dump body. *American Truck Historical Society*

Chapter Five

Wartime Horsepower
1941–1950

Most deliveries of commercial trucks for non-military uses stopped in early 1942 and did not resume until late in 1945 following the end of World War II. Gasoline and tires were rationed during the war and several breweries returned to the use of horses and horse-drawn wagons for making local deliveries. Truck models remained unchanged until about 1948, when some new postwar designs were released.

An article in an Anheuser-Busch's 1941 house organ commented on the role of trucking:

> Important chapters of Budweiser's success story are being written by these powerful carriers who transport our beers as far away as 700 miles from the brewery. Before Prohibition, Budweiser wholesalers shipped by railroad only. Today, transport trucks carry one-fifth of all the beer brewed by Anheuser-Busch. Better trucks and better highways are the answer. And with America's thirst for progress, trucking hauls of 1000 miles and more are in prospect.
>
> Many truck-trailer units carrying Budweiser were covering 500,000 to 750,000 miles annually. Many wholesalers had begun purchasing diesel units before the United States became involved in World War II.

A study of the industry in *American Brewing Industry and the Beer Market*, by Shih and Shih, tallied the types of containers in which beer was distributed in 1947. Total production was 87 million barrels. Of this, 32 percent was draught beer that was distributed in

A 1941 Chevrolet used by the Grand Island, Nebraska, distributor for Falstaff beer. *Omaha Body & Equipment Company*

barrels. Returnable bottles accounted for 66 percent; non-returnable bottles and cans accounted for just under one percent each.

By 1950, rankings of the nation's 10 largest brewers had changed. In descending order of popularity they were Schlitz, Anheuser-Busch, Ballantine, Pabst, Schaefer, Liebmann, Falstaff, Miller, Blatz, and Pfeiffer. The top 10 controlled 38 percent of the market. The top 10 beer-producing states, in descending order, were Wisconsin, New York, Pennsylvania, Missouri, New Jersey, Ohio, Illinois, California, Michigan, and Minnesota.

An early-1940s Diamond-T powered with butane gas. Eastside beer was brewed in Los Angeles. The truck has California plates. *Bill West*

Gluek's beer was carried in this early-1940s Dodge cab-over. *Omaha Body & Equipment Company*

This 1942 Mack tractor with semitrailer was used by the Hamtramck, New Jersey, distributor of Pfeiffer's.

A 1940s Dodge COE with a Heiser body that carried Miller High Life. *Geo. Heiser Body Company*

A Chicago distributor of Kingsbury beer used this 1946 White. Kingsbury beer was brewed in Sheboygan, Wisconsin. *American Truck Historical Society*

Mitchell's Premium beer is distributed in an insulated semitrailer, pulled by a 1940s White tractor in El Paso, Texas. The truck has 1946 plates. *American Truck Historical Society*

A White tractor with a sleeper cab, from just after World War II, with a semitrailer carrying Atlantic beer and ale. *American Truck Historical Society*

A 1946 White with Ohio plates, used by an Erin Brew distributor. The body is insulated. *American Truck Historical Society*

A 1947 Autocar COE used by the Peter Fox Brewing Company of Chicago for carrying Fox DeLuxe beer. *W. A. Drew*

There's a Heiser body on this postwar International that carried Bohemian Pale beer. *Geo. Heiser Body Company*

This 1947 Mack was photographed in Paterson, New Jersey, delivering Schaefer beer. The Schaefer Brewing Company had breweries in Albany and Brooklyn, New York. *William J. Wright*

This 1940s White with a 1947 Pennsylvania license plate carries cases of Fort Pitt beer. The body is shaped like a dump body although no lifting mechanism is visible. The sign on the door advertises Old Shay ale. Fort Pitt beer was brewed in Pittsburgh. *American Truck Historical Society*

Grand Prize beer was carried in this Fruehauf trailer behind a White tractor. The tractor has 1947 Texas plates. *American Truck Historical Society*

Molson's is a Canadian beer. The truck is a White, from the 1940s. *American Truck Historical Society*

This postwar White tractor with a Fruehauf semi-trailer carried Falls City beer for a distributor in Huntington, West Virginia. Falls City was brewed in Louisville. *American Truck Historical Society*

A Chicago distributor of Atlas Prager used this 1947 White. Note the platform above the cab roof on which the worker is standing. There may be a ladder on the far side to allow him to reach the cab's roof. Atlas beer was brewed in Chicago. *American Truck Historical Society*

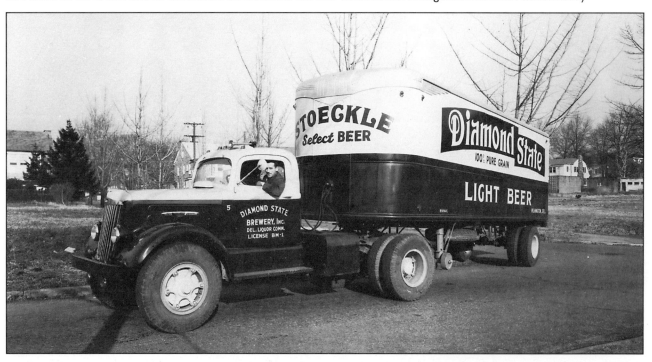

Delaware's Diamond State Brewery used this postwar White for hauling Stoeckle Select and Diamond State beers. *American Truck Historical Society*

Ruppert Knickerbocker beer carried in a Trailmobile semitrailer, pulled by a late-1940s White tractor. Barely visible in front of the tractor's rear wheel is a sander that drops grit in front of the tire when needed. *American Truck Historical Society*

A late-1940s International used by a distributor of Stag beer located in Independence, Missouri. *Pullman Trailmobile*

A late-1940s Kenworth powered with a Hall Scott butane-powered engine. It's pulling both a semitrailer and a full trailer of Regal Pale. *Bill West*

Rheingold beer was carried in Brooklyn in this 1940s White. From 1940 to 1965 the company sponsored a "Miss Rheingold" beauty contest. *American Truck Historical Society*

A fleet of late-1940s Whites used to distribute Lone Star beer, brewed in San Antonio, Texas. *American Truck Historical Society*

The Coca-Cola distributor in Austin, Minnesota, used this 1949 Chevrolet for carrying Hamm's beer. *Kolstad Company*

A Heiser body on a late-1940s Ford used by a Sicks' Select distributor. Sicks' was brewed in Seattle. *Geo. Heiser Body Company*

A 1948–1950 Ford tractor and semitrailer with a load of Miller beer. *Pullman Trailmobile*

A 1949 International parked in front of a dealership, waiting to be picked up by a southern Colorado distributor of Coors. *Adolph Coors Company*

Gunther beer was carried in these late-1940s Whites for distributing in Miami. Bodies were built by Fruehauf. *American Truck Historical Society*

Loading barrels of Weber Waukesha beer into a late-1940s White. *American Truck Historical Society*

Buckeye Distributors used this 1949 White COE. Note the white side curtains and two-wheel dollies. The beer is Carlings Black Label. *American Truck Historical Society*

The purpose of the flowers is unclear. The truck is a 1949 White used by the Genesee Brewing Company in Rochester, New York.
American Truck Historical Society

Heidelberg beer was brewed in Tacoma, Washington, and distributed in the Salem, Oregon, area using this late-1940s White. The forklift is moving a palletload. *American Truck Historical Society*

The sign on the trailer's side proclaims: "Another load of Muehlebach Beer for Dallas." The truck is a 1949 White. The light truck color helped reflect the sun. *American Truck Historical Society*

Regal Pale beer was brewed in San Francisco and distributed in Oakland, California, in this late-1940s White. *American Truck Historical Society*

A 1950 White used in Arnold, Pennsylvania, for distributing Iron City and Dutch Club beers. Note the striped bumper. *American Truck Historical Society*

Wiedemann's beer was brewed in Newport, Kentucky, and is shown in a circa-1950 White. The front stack of cases is on a pallet, presumably loaded with a forklift. *American Truck Historical Society*

A beer distributor in Alexandria, Virginia, used this circa-1950 White cab-over for distributing Valley Forge beer. Note that a step extends along the entire bottom edge of the body. *American Truck Historical Society*

Old Dutch beer was distributed in Toledo, Ohio, using this circa-1950 White. The beer was brewed by the Krantz Brewing Corporation of Toledo. *American Truck Historical Society*

Delivering barrels of Golden Hudepohl beer from a circa-1950 White. The truck body has gates that open to the side, and the load is also protected by a light-colored tarp. Hudepohl beer was brewed in Cincinnati. *American Truck Historical Society*

A circa-1950 White COE carrying Champagne Velvet beer. *American Truck Historical Society*

A circa-1950 White truck used by the Cleveland Sandusky Brewing Corporation to deliver Gold Bond Beer. *American Truck Historical Society*

An insulated body on a circa-1950 White used in New Orleans. The product was Regal beer. *American Truck Historical Society*

Chapter Six

Distribution Goes National
1951–1960

Television was introduced to many American households during the decade 1951–1961. This would be of some significance to the beer industry, since breweries realized that if they were to obtain full benefits from advertising on national TV, they would have to distribute their product on a nationwide basis. Hence, the larger brewers began to expand. From a transportation standpoint, rail would be continued to be used for many beer shipments because of the weight. Trucks would be used to deliver the beer from the distributor's warehouse and for shorter city-to-city hauls.

In the postwar years, the number of truck manufacturers consolidated and would remain steady until imports appeared in the late 1970s. A beer truck relied on two manufacturers: the chassis builder, such as Dodge or Chevrolet, and a body builder.

A 1951 Autocar used by the Taunton, Massachusetts, distributor of Narragansett beer, which was brewed in Cranston, Rhode Island. The advertising slogan painted on both front and side said: "Hi neighbor! have a 'Gansett." *American Truck Historical Society*

Ready for parade duty is this early-1950s Dodge COE, which is promoting Altes Lager beer. On top of the cab are four loud-speakers. *National Automotive History Collection, Detroit Public Library*

For Chevrolet truck buyers, the catalog was called *The Silver Book*. The 1954 catalog listed the following firms as builders and suppliers of beer bodies: Brown Trailers, Inc., Toledo; DeKalb Commercial Body Corporation, DeKalb, Illinois; Fruehauf Trailer Company, Detroit; General Body Manufacturing Company, Kansas City, Missouri; Hackney Brothers Body Company, Wilson, North Carolina; Herman Body Company, St. Louis; Hesse Carriage Company, Kansas City, Missouri; McCabe-Powers Auto Body Company, St. Louis; Mid-West Body & Manufacturing, Paris, Illinois; Omaha Body & Equipment Company, Inc., Omaha; Proctor-Keefe Body Company, Inc., Detroit; The Schnable Company, Pittsburgh; and Universal Sales, Inc., Delaware, Ohio.

Red Hook Brewery in Seattle currently uses this 1951 Ford panel for promotional work. It's shown at a shopping center parking lot promotional display. The truck originated in Richland, Washington, and later was used by a caterer in the Seattle Public Market. *Chris Hem*

Body builders were located in nearly every community, and many could trace their origins to wagon building. Truck-body building was somewhat localized because the completed truck body was quite bulky and expensive to ship long distances. The beer distributor then would have to buy both a truck and a body. If he preferred a certain make of truck, the truck dealer would also have a catalog that contained ads from various body builders who could supply and fit a body to his truck.

The new truck's chassis and cab would be delivered directly to the body builder who would build and attach the body to the chassis. He would also paint the body and add any decals supplied by the brewer and do any lettering that the buyer requested.

The Shih and Shih study of the industry concluded that in the late 1950s there were 234 brewers operating 260 breweries and using 6,000 distributors to reach 170,000 beer outlets. Milwaukee was the

Koehler's beer was distributed in Erie, using this early 1950s White cab-over. Note that the stacks of loaded cases slope inward. This contributed to load stability when turning corners. *American Truck Historical Society*

nation's largest producer of beer, followed by New York, Detroit, Newark, St. Louis, San Francisco, Los Angeles, Minneapolis/St. Paul, and Philadelphia.

The same study also looked at the seasonality of beer sales, always a vexing problem for distributors since the demand was uneven. According to the study of the period from 1947–1957, if we consider 100 percent as the "average" month (annual shipments divided by 12) here's how each month compared: January, 81 percent; February, 78 percent; March, 93 percent; April, 97 percent; May, 106 percent; June, 119 percent; July, 125 percent; August, 123 percent; September, 105 percent; October, 96 percent; November, 87 percent; and December, 90 percent. Hence, in August, the distributor would be one and one-half times as busy as in February.

Shih and Shih tallied the types of containers in which beer was distributed in 1957. Total production was 84

million barrels, down slightly from a decade earlier. Of this, 21 percent was draught beer and distributed in barrels. Returnable bottles accounted for 46 percent; nonreturnable bottles, 4 percent; and canned beer, 29 percent.

Rankings of brewers continued to shift. By 1957, the 10 most popular in descending order were Anheuser-Busch, Schlitz, Falstaff, Ballantine, Hamm's, Carling, Liebmann, Pabst, Schaefer, and Stroh. The top 10 controlled 46 percent of the market. Hamm's, Carling, and Falstaff still did not have nationwide distribution. The next fifteen brewers, still in descending order, were Miller, Lucky Lager, C. Schmidt, Ruppert, Piel Brothers, Drewerys, National, Blatz, Coors, Jackson, Olympia, Duquesne, Burgermeister, Pearl, and Pfeiffer.

Coors introduced the two-piece aluminum cans and also began a recycling plant. Aluminum cans changed the transportation characteristics of beer since they resulted in a much denser pack.

A circa-1950 White tractor and large trailer used by a Brooklyn-based Rheingold beer distributor. At the far left of the trailer side is the firm's state brewers' license number, no doubt required by strict state regulations. *Grumman Aerospace Corporation*

Ad for an early side-loading pallet-carrying beer body built by Herman. The truck is an early-1950s GMC COE. *Hewitt-Lucas Body Co.*

Only a few pictures were found of beer being shipped in tank trucks or railroad tank cars in the United States, as was this load of beer carried in a tank truck in Ireland. The product is Guinness and the truck is a 1950s Leyland. In the 1950s, Guinness also had a fleet of barges and ocean-going ships that carried its product in casks and 504-gallon portable tanks. *Guinness Archives*

A 1950s Peugeot, spotted in Amsterdam in 1997, used to promote Mexican Corona beer. The Corona sign is not visible from this angle.

A 1952 White COE with Wisconsin plates, used to distribute Gettelman beer. Slogan "Get Get Gettelman" is painted on side.
American Truck Historical Society

This 1952 photo shows three new trucks used by a Miller distributor in Chicago. The small Ford on the left would have been used for sales and promotion. The Ford in the center and the White were used for deliveries. *Miller Brewing Company*

Three Whites from the early 1950s used to deliver P. O. C. Pilsener beer. *American Truck Historical Society*

An attractively signed body built by Heiser for a Rainier distributor. The chassis is an early-1950s White. *Geo. Heiser Body Co.*

Sicks' Century brews were hauled in this early-1950s Ford with a Heiser body. *Geo. Heiser Body Company*

A circa-1953 White with a load of Ballantine beer and ale. A Chevrolet and Ford are visible in the background. *American Truck Historical Society*

A 1953 White tractor with a semitrailer owned by the Duquesne Brewing Company of Pittsburgh, Pennsylvania. The sign on the side extols Silver Top beer. *American Truck Historical Society*

A small beer body, built by Hewitt-Lucas Body Company, mounted on a mid-1950s Ford step-van chassis. *Hewitt-Lucas Body Company*

A mid-1950s GMC with twin rear axles and a Kolstad body used for hauling Hamm's. *Kolstad Company*

A mid-1950s International carrying Hauenstein New Ulm Beer, brewed in New Ulm, Minnesota. Note the tailgate platform, unusual in beer trucks. *Kolstad Company*

The Guinness truck maintenance shop in the 1950s. *Guinness Archives*

A 1956 Chevrolet with a Marion body outfitted to haul Hamm's Beer. *Marion Body Co.*

A fleet of National Bohemian beer trucks. The lead truck is a 1956 International, followed by a GMC. *W. F. Mickey Body Company, Inc.*

A picture of a Stroh's loading dock in the mid-1950s. From left to right are an International, two Whites, a Dodge, two more Whites (one with Goebel markings), a Ford, and an Autocar. *Stroh Brewing Company*

Redtop Brewing Company, in Cincinnati, used this 1956 White tractor with semitrailer. *American Truck Historical Society*

A 1957 GMC with a Reliance body used by a northern California distributor of Burgermeister, which was brewed in San Francisco. *Daily Body Company*

A 1958 Chevrolet with twin headlights and a Hesse body, carrying Hamm's beer for a Kansas City, Missouri, distributor. The body has sliding doors visible on this side. The Hesse firm can trace its lineage back to a blacksmith shop in Leavenworth, Kansas, in 1847. *Hesse Corporation*

A Hesse body with a refrigeration unit on a Ford C-series chassis, circa 1960. The truck was operated by the Coors distributor in Craig, Colorado. Coors made a point of having its beer cooled for its entire trip to the consumer and advertised that fact. *Hesse Corporation*

Chapter Seven

99 Bottles of Beer on the Truck
1961–1970

Major breweries continued to develop nationwide markets. This helped the rail industry more than trucks, since beer, because of its heavy weight and uniform packaging, is an ideal railroad cargo for distances beyond several hundred miles. Indeed, we do not see many trucks carrying full loads of beer between major cities; beer trucks spotted in rural areas are usually making local deliveries to retail stores and to clubs and taverns along their route.

Within the United States in 1967, 38.1 percent of beer was shipped in cans, 45.8 percent in bottles, and 16.1 percent in kegs and barrels. Some breweries began using shorter bottles without necks (called "shorties" or "stubbies"). They were not popular with consumers, even though they had more favorable shipping characteristics than the conventional long-necked beer bottles. Taverns that sold bottled beer still collected and returned the empty bottles and cases. For beer consumed at home, the cans or bottles were usually discarded as part of that household's trash and ended up in the city dump.

In addition to the large trucks that carried beer in barrels, cans, and bottles, distributors also used smaller trucks. For large customers, the sales might be separate from deliveries, and the small truck would be used by a salesman, who would take the order and have it delivered on the following day. The salesman often had additional promotional materials to hand out to bars and restaurant. The most common was the enameled serving tray, 12 to 13 inches in diameter, with the brewery's name, logo, and other artwork. (One beer enthusiasts' book shows a tray distributed by the Star Brewing Company in Boston with a picture of an early 1930s Autocar carrying barrels of Star beer.) Other promotional materials included calendars, posters, tap knobs, glasses, mugs, metal signs, napkins, coasters, and neon signs.

An early-1960s Dodge with a short trailer, in front of the W. F. Mickey Body Company factory. The truck has Pabst markings. The side doors on the truck body roll up past the top edge of the roof of the body, making it easier to use a lift truck for loading pallets. *W. F. Mickey Body Company, Inc.*

A Mickey body on an early-1960s GMC chassis. *W. F. Mickey Body Company, Inc.*

The 1968 edition of *The Silver Book* carried ads for the following beer truck body and trailer makers: Boyertown Auto Body Works, Inc., Boyertown, Pennsylvania; Brunswick Corporation, Muskegon, Michigan; A. Cresci & Son, Inc., Vineland, New Jersey; DeKalb Commercial Body Corp.; Fruehauf; Lyncoach & Truck Co., Inc., Oneonta, New York; McCabe Powers Body Co.; Mid-West Body & Manufacturing; J. B. E. Olson Corporation, Garden City, New York; Penn Trailers & Truck Bodies, Chicago; and Pierce Auto Body Works, Appleton, Wisconsin. The firms were listed under one or more of the following categories: beer delivery—sliding door, or beer delivery—pallet-loading.

A Dailey body built for a Miller distributor on a 1963 GMC cab-over. *Dailey Body Company*

On the Dailey-built body, side doors open up high to allow filling of bays with a forklift. An industry source in the 1970s reported that the use of bays increased a driver's productivity by 4 to 11 percent. *Dailey Body Company*

Lucky Lager carried in a White Freightliner tractor/semitrailer. *Bob Koprivica, Jr.*

A 1960s White carrying Moosehead beer in Canada. The trailer has a refrigeration unit. *Moosehead Breweries, Ltd.*

A 1966 Ford C-series, with a new Heiser body, destined for a Michelob distributor. *Geo. Heiser Body Company*

A mid-1960s International outside the Heiser Body Company plant in Seattle. The body had a sliding door on each side and an overhead door in the rear. The buyer was the local Olympia distributor. *Geo. Heiser Body Company*

Brew 66 was carried on this 1967 Ford with a Heiser body. *Geo. Heiser Body Company*

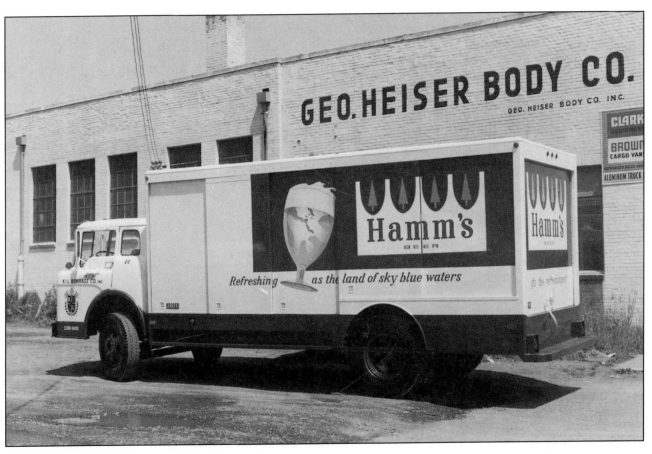

Heiser truck bodies are built in Seattle. This 10-bay body is mounted on a late-1960s Ford C series, and carried Hamm's. *Geo. Heiser Body Company*

A 1967 Ford used by the Port Angeles, Washington, distributor for Schlitz. The body was built by Heiser. *Geo. Heiser Body Company*

This mid-1960s Freightliner, with a Heiser body, distributed Olympia beer in Fairbanks, Alaska. *Geo. Heiser Body Company*

A 1969 GMC tractor with a Hesse 12-bay trailer made for carrying Budweiser. *Hesse Corporation*

This late-1960s White carried palletloads of Schaefer's beer in Brooklyn, New York. Note that with the doors to the side bays open, one can see through the body. *American Truck Historical Society*

Chapter Eight

Consolidation and Imports
1971–1980

There were many brewery mergers during the decade 1971–1980. Pabst bought Blatz and Heileman bought Rainier, Grain Belt, Falls City, and Carling. Olympia bought Hamm's and Lone Star; Schmidt bought Rheingold, Duquesne, and Ortlieb. Stroh acquired Schaefer. The names of the acquired brands did not always disappear since they had value in their existing local markets. By 1976, four major breweries controlled about 60 percent of the nation's beer sales. They were Anheuser-Busch, Schlitz, Miller, and Pabst. Trailing these were Coors, Olympia, Stroh, Schaefer, Heileman, Carling, Falstaff, Schmidt, Genesee, and

Pearl. Combined, these 14 breweries controlled 94 percent of beer sales.

As domestic breweries consolidated, import beers began moving into U.S. markets. A 1982 report, "The Beer Industry, A Comprehensive Review and Analysis," listed these 1980 imports, in descending order. Heineken (which accounted for over 1/3 of all exports), Molson, Beck's, Labatt's, Moosehead, Dos Equis, St. Pauli Girl, Foster's Lager, and Guiness.

While breweries consolidated, they also increased the number of different brands they offered. "Lite" beers would be one example. One reason for introducing

Doors are yet to be added to this Hesse body. Three of the bays would accommodate two palletloads apiece. The chassis is a 1971 Chevrolet COE. *Hesse Corporation*

A Kranz body on a circa-1970 Ford C-series, used to carry Carling Black Label and Stag beer. *Kranz Automotive Body Company*

additional brands was to gain shelf space in retail outlets (known in marketing as "product proliferation"). Hence the same truck that once carried only 1 or 2 types of beer would now be carrying 8 to 10. This made it difficult for the driver/salesman to plan his load, so distributors went to a "pre-sell" operation.

In preselling, the distributor's salesperson calls on the retailer, makes a sales pitch, hangs an advertising sign or two, and then takes an order. The order would then be delivered the following day by a driver whose sole task was to make deliveries. The driver/salesmen were phased out.

Some brewers began advertising the fact that their product was continuously refrigerated from the time it was produced until it was sold at the retail outlet.

In 1972, over half (53.2 percent) of beer was shipped in cans, 34.7 percent in bottles, and 12.1 percent in kegs and barrels. Nonreturnable beer bottles were almost as numerous as returnable ones; the shift away from returnables reduced the driver/salesman's task of picking up returns. Nonreturnables did add to the amount of litter that property owners and cities had to contend with.

The several fuel crises of the decade produced spot shortages of fuel and drove up fuel prices and delivery costs. It also encouraged the use of more aluminum, which is lighter than steel. One industry source at that time said that an aluminum beverage body 22 feet long weighed the same as a steel body that was 20 feet long. Aluminum bodies also had fewer problems with salt used on highways in northern climates. Diesel engines, coupled with automatic transmissions were widely used and, in the late 1970s, each diesel engine manufacturer came out with a more fuel-efficient model. The automatic transmissions reduced driver fatigue (of special concern to route-salesmen) and resulted in less wear and tear on the truck.

Hackney Brothers' beverage-body literature included a one-sheet insert that said their body design's rounded corners cut fuel consumption by as much as 15 percent. Diagrams showed how the rounded corners reduced the drag along both the sides and the top. Wind deflectors were placed on the tops of cabs, and the flat fronts of trailers had a "bubble" design added to help deflect the wind.

Another development was the swan-necked trailer, pulled on a fifth-wheel device mounted in the box of a 3/4-ton or larger pickup. The trailer had two axles and its tires were relatively small, often smaller than the tires on the pickup. They apparently were not to be used for highway hauling but could be used for local

A mid-1970s Ford chassis with a Hesse body used to distribute Schlitz Encore beer. *Hesse Corporation*

deliveries. They apparently were less expensive than a conventional medium- or heavy-duty truck with the same capacity. The advantage of a fleet of trucks with trailers over a fleet of straight trucks is that the distributor could have more trailers than trucks and could be loading trailers with product at the warehouse, while other trailers were being delivered.

In the rear is a 1975 International, in the front, a 1927 International—both are used to market Old Chicago beer. *American Automobile Manufacturers Assn.*

Schlitz Malt Liquor was carried in this 1970s Ford C-series with a Hesse body. The truck was painted white, with the trim and signs in blue. *Hesse Corporation*

A Hesse 10-bay body on a Ford C-series chassis, outfitted to carry Busch Bavarian. *Hesse Corporation*

An enclosed beverage body on a 1977 Ford chassis. *West Coast Beverage Sales*

A Hesse aluminum body on an early-1970s Ford used for hauling Piels beer. *Hesse Corporation*

A late-1970s International tractor with Coors markings pulls an intermodal (truck/rail/ocean) container with Matson markings. Matson is an ocean carrier that operates between the West Coast of the United States and Hawaii. Mark R. Wayman

Mark Body, of Mt. Clemens, Michigan, built this aluminum body for a Blatz distributor on a late-1970s International chassis. The bar in front of the rear wheel is for the driver to stand on when unloading the bay above the rear axle. *Mark Body*

Chapter Nine

Big Trucks, Lite Beer, and Microbreweries
1981–Today

The 1980s and 1990s have yielded ongoing developments, affecting the way beer is distributed and the trucks that deliver it.

"Lite" beers, introduced in the late 1970s, continued to increase their market share. Most were variants of well-known national brands and were distributed through the same channels. Brewers also introduced fancy and premium brands and ales that met with varied success. As noted before, brewers introduced new brands in part to command more space in retail outlets.

According to Bob Koprivica, Jr., a former beer distributor in the Pacific Northwest, beer trucks have

A Ford with a "productmobile" body consisting of a large six-pack of Sharps beer. The refrigeration units can be seen. Some bodies like this open up and have beer taps for dispensing beer.

An early-1980s aluminum route trailer with 16 bays, built by Mark Body. It was equipped with a central locking system. *Mark Body*

A Coor's distributor in Reno, Nevada used this 1984 Chevrolet for his sales force. Note the roof.

changed because beer consumers are buying less beer in taverns, restaurants, and nightclubs and buying more beer in supermarkets, mass merchandisers, convenience stores, and liquor stores. Beer used to be delivered almost exclusively on low-slung, side-loading/unloading trucks. With the shift in consumer purchasing patterns, more distributorships are converting their fleets to rear loading/unloading trucks which enable the driver to unload at dock level at retail accounts, using a forklift or pallet jack.

More distributors transferred many of their sales and delivery systems to pre-sell, especially for larger accounts. This yielded a more efficient use of trucks, since they carried only what had been ordered and did not have to remain idle while the driver/salesman made his sales pitch and handled paperwork.

In other situations, driver/salesmen are used on some distribution routes. They are equipped with hand-held computers, which generate the sales invoice, sales tracking, and inventory-adjustment records. Individuals pre-selling also use hand-held computers and devices that have the capability of transmitting the order back to the distributor by radio, initiating order-picking instructions and sometimes triggering same-day delivery.

Some states had programs that encouraged use of returnable containers, or at least their recycling. Michigan, for example, began to collect a 10-cent deposit on all bottles and cans to encourage people to return them to the store to be picked up by the distributor. In Canada, Labatt claims that 98 percent of all bottles are returned, as are over 95 percent of all other packing materials. Returnable bottles work their way back through the brewers' and distributors' systems, while generalized recycling systems may mean only that the bottle or can is collected, ground up or melted, and then used to make a new container.

Microbreweries started springing up and, in a sense, reintroduced the concept of "local" brews and breweries. By 1994, microbrews accounted for nearly 10 percent of the beers sold in the United States. At first their need for trucks was slight since they sold only in their taproom. According to Dick King, the owner of the New England Brewing Company of Norwalk, Connecticut, they started with a single Toyota pickup

A mid-1980s GMC distributing Miller in Madison, Wisconsin. Note the add-on extension to the front bumper, making it lower.

equipped with an air-conditioned box. The chassis has been replaced twice. The body has taps and is used mainly for special events and promotions, he says.

New England Brewing has since purchased an Isuzu NPR truck and fitted it with an insulated body. With 160,000 miles, it's proven reliable, and the drivers find the low cab-forward design easy to maneuver in city driving. The company also owns a medium-sized Mack, and three Ford Ranger pickups for use by its sales force.

Age Dating

Many brewers began "dating" their beer so that it was necessary for distributors and retailers to use FIFO (first-in, first-out) inventory management systems. One anecdote concerning the speed with which beer flowed through the distribution channels appeared on the worldwide web in August 1997. A late afternoon beer drinker in Loughmillers, an Indianapolis pub, noted that his can of Budweiser was dated with the "born on" date that was the very same day on which he was drinking it. He checked with the local Anheuser-

Busch distributor who said that it was possible. The beer had been produced in Columbus, Ohio. The brewery was operating 24 hours a day (this was mid-summer). According to the distributor,

> Anywhere from eight to twenty big ol' beer trucks roll out of Columbus for Indianapolis every day. At least three of them are loaded with nothing but Budweiser in the 24-can loose pack cases. If one of those trucks rolled toward Indianapolis early that morning, and Loughmiller's received a delivery that afternoon, then it is entirely plausible for a Hoosier to be gulping Bud on the very day that it was born.

On the subject of dating beer, Coors reportedly requires its distributors to "pull" packaged beer not sold within 112 days. Kegs of beer must be pulled within 45 to 60 days.

More refrigerated and insulated bodies are in use because beer is moving though distribution channels more expeditiously and retailers prefer receiving beer that is already cooled, since that's what many of their customers also want. Trucks have side-loading bays and

A mid-1980s Mack spotted in Wisconsin Dells, Wisconsin. It was used by a Miller distributor. The front bay has cases, the rear, kegs.

some have only certain bays refrigerated; removable insulated liners could be placed in specific bays as needed. (In winter climates, the insulation is sometimes needed to keep beer from freezing. Some enclosed beer bodies actually come with heating devices.) If the beer is not cool when the retailer receives it, it must be placed in the back-room cooler before being sold.

A 1997 report on market shares indicated that Anheuser-Busch controlled 46.5 percent, followed by Miller, with 22.3 percent, Coors, 10 percent, and Stroh's 7.8 percent. Over half of Anheuser-Busch's sales are of Budweiser. Imports continued to grow. The *Journal of Commerce*, a maritime newspaper, reported in its November 6, 1998, edition that:

> One out of every eight [ocean-going] containers arriving from Northern European countries contains beer, underscoring the established presence of Heineken, Guinness, Amstel and other European brands in the American market. . . . Beer imports in the first six months of 1998 surged by 110 percent from Belgium, 84 percent from Ireland and 40.4 percent from Britain. . . .

In late 1998, Miller began test-marketing beer in plastic bottles. The intended market would be mainly sports arenas where tap beer is presently served in plastic cups rather than glass bottles (which can be used as missiles in case one disagrees with an official's call). In other trades, substitution of plastic for glass has resulted in weight savings.

Few immediate changes are expected for beer trucks operating early in the next century. Size, weight, and axle-spacing rules are in effect and not expected to change. The beer-distribution network is also in place and distributors will resist most changes. Deliveries of refrigerated, packaged beer to retailers will increase because products move through the supply chain so quickly—nobody wants the responsibility for holding the inventory while it's waiting to be cooled.

A late-1980s Ford carrying Schlitz malt liquor, and operated by the J. W. Costello Beverage Company, of Las Vegas, Nevada. *Mark R. Wayman*

Oldenberg Brewing Company, in Fort Mitchell, Kentucky, uses this "replicar" that is supposed to look like an early-1930s REO. It was built on a 1987 GMC chassis and has an Oldsmobile diesel engine. Is also has an automatic transmission and power steering. The body is refrigerated and can hold 21 half-barrels. On the right side the body opens up to expose six beer taps. The truck builder was Cook Brothers, a firm in Elsmere, Kentucky. *Oldenberg Brewing Company*

A late-1980s International tractor with a sleeper cab and long semitrailer used in Nevada. *Mark R. Wayman*

A late-1980s International, with Red Dog markings, owned by a Green Bay, Wisconsin, distributor.

Old Dominion Brewing Company is a microbrewery established in Ashburn, Virginia, in 1989. Their truck is a 1989 Mitsubishi with its body built and installed by the Morgan Corporation of Morgantown, Pennsylvania. *Old Dominion Brewing Company*

Note the large Miller decals on the side of this trailer photographed in Racine, Wisconsin, in 1998. The tractor is a circa-1990 International.

Unloading several different brands of beer from a semitrailer with a pallet-jack. The pallet-loads are covered by shrink-wrap. *Hesse Corporation*

Bud Light markings on an early-1990s Freightliner tractor with a semitrailer that operated in Nevada. *Mark R. Wayman*

Imported Heineken was featured on this early-1990s International used by a Nevada distributor. *Mark R. Wayman*

This is a tractor (probably an early-1990s Peterbilt) pulling two semitrailers (the second one on a dolly) used by a Nevada Budweiser distributor. This particular rig was used to make retail deliveries outside of urban areas. Both trailers had side bays for holding the product. *Mark R. Wayman*

A 1993 International tractor with Miller Lite markings on the Hesse trailer. *Hesse Corporation*

A 1994 Ford with Coors markings, spotted at a Eureka, California, convenience store/filling station site.

A mid-1990s Freightliner makes a delivery of Budweiser in Kenosha, Wisconsin.

A 1994 International with a load of Moosehead Dry. *Moosehead Breweries, Ltd.*

A 1994 Kenworth tractor in the Olympia Brewing lot in Olympia, Washington. Trailers in background have Pabst, Hamms, and Lucky Lager markings. Lettering on the tractor's wind deflector reads "General Brewing Company."

Bavaria beer, brewed in the Netherlands, is carried on this DAF truck-trailer. *Bavaria*

A mid-1990s Ford pulling a trailer with Coors markings spotted at a "Beerfest" in San Jose, California. It has a refrigeration unit and was being used to keep the reserve inventory of beer cool until it was needed at the sales booth.

A relatively small mid-1990s GMC, used by an Eau Claire, Wisconsin, Anheuser-Busch distributor for serving rural areas.

A mid-1990s GMC Sonoma used by the sales force of a Madison, Wisconsin, Budweiser distributor.

A Mercedes, carrying Belgish Abdijbier in the Netherlands. *Interbrew*

A trailer used by a Budweiser distributor for dispensing beer at outdoor events. Note the taps and sink/tray.

A European-spec Volvo with a load of
Amstel beer. *Heineken Nederland B.O.*

Beamish Irish Stout in kegs is carried on
a DAF, spotted in Ireland in 1997.

A small European Ford used by a Miller distributor in Cork
City, Ireland. The sales rep is using her cellular phone.

A Miller distributor, in San Rafael, California, used this late-1990s GMC Safari panel truck for supplying a small-town festival in Tomales, California.

A Volvo truck, pulling a full trailer, used in the Netherlands for carrying Oranjeboom. *Interbrew*

The Waymatic Company, of Fulton, Kentucky, makes beer-dispensing trailers. They are equipped to keep beer cold and to dispense it from the side or rear. Some are equipped to open into various counter arrangements. They are used at fairs, tractor pulls, and other similar events. The firm also makes beer-dispensing truck bodies. *Waymatic*

A DAF tractor, with a pull down side-curtain, hauling a load of Dommelsch beer. *Interbrew*

The brewers provide stencils, and today the sides of many beer trucks are completely covered with advertising. Localized stencils can also be applied. This one recognizes the accomplishments of the Green Bay Packers and, fittingly, was spotted near Green Bay, Wisconsin. Note the two-wheel dolly hanging on rear.

HACKNEY BODIES

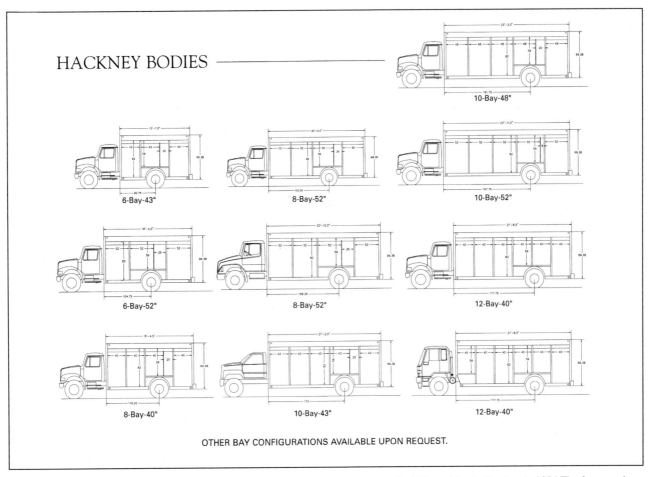

10-Bay-48"

6-Bay-43"   8-Bay-52"   10-Bay-52"

6-Bay-52"   8-Bay-52"   12-Bay-40"

8-Bay-40"   10-Bay-43"   12-Bay-40"

OTHER BAY CONFIGURATIONS AVAILABLE UPON REQUEST.

These are many of the beverage bodies for trucks built by Hackney, a firm that started in Wilson, North Carolina, in 1854. The firm was best known for its bus bodies and its refrigerated bodies. The same literature showed pictures of additional bodies for smaller trucks, semitrailers, and a double trailer. Some bodies were equipped with mechanical refrigeration and some had only certain bays refrigerated. *Hackne*

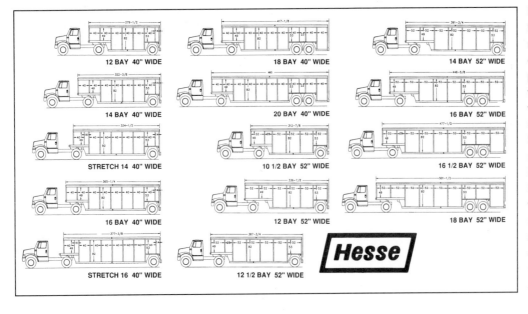

12 BAY 40" WIDE   18 BAY 40" WIDE   14 BAY 52" WIDE

14 BAY 40" WIDE   20 BAY 40" WIDE   16 BAY 52" WIDE

STRETCH 14 40" WIDE   10 1/2 BAY 52" WIDE   16 1/2 BAY 52" WIDE

16 BAY 40" WIDE   12 BAY 52" WIDE   18 BAY 52" WIDE

STRETCH 16 40" WIDE   12 1/2 BAY 52" WIDE   **Hesse**

Hesse, of Kansas City, Missouri, manufactures a range of beer semitrailers, with many of them pictured here. All load from the side and the bay width can be either 40 inches or 52 inches. The bodies are made of aluminum. Note that some have a fractional, or small bay. That's usually used for carrying promotional materials or cases of special brews—such as some exports—that move in small quantities. *Hesse Corporation*

Bibliography

"A Big Brewery Power Wagon Equipment." *The Western Brewer and Journal of the Barley, Malt and Hop Trade* (February 1912): 73–77.

"A World on Wheels." *A-B Ink* (September 1941): 8–9.

"Adolph Coors Company, The." (http://mason.gmu.edu/~rsisodia/student/coors.htm).

American Beer Industry, The: an economic, marketing, and financial investigation, Merrick, N.Y.: The Morton Research Group, 1978.

American Body & Equipment Company literature, various dates.

"Anheuser-Busch Truck Bodies," *Bevo Tatler* (January 1921): 6–7.

Anderson, Will. *The Beer Book*. Philadelphia: Pearl Pressman-Liberty, 1973.

Beer Wholesalers: Who Are They? Alexandria, Virginia: National Beer Wholesalers Associations, ca. 1996.

Brewing Industry, The New York: William B. Nichols & Co., 1933.

"Delivering the Goodness," *The Guinness Harp* (September/November 1958): 4–5.

Draught Beer in Metropolitan Toronto. Ottawa: Restrictive Trade Practices Commission, 1972.

"Ford—a Complete Line of Trucks and Commercial Cars for the Brewing Industry." Sales literature, circa 1933.

Geiger, C. W. "Low-Bed Trucks for Unloading Keg Beer." *Power Wagon*. (September 1937).

Hackney literature, various dates.

Hesse literature, various dates.

Hewitt-Lucas Body Co. literature, various dates.

"History of Beer in California, The." (http:www.ncbev.com/cahist.htm).

Hobbs literature, various dates.

Hook, George T. "Trucks Meet 3.2 Percent Beer Hauling Problems 100 Percent." *The Commercial Car Journal.* (April 1933): 10–13.

Howey, Brian A. "Rapid transit on the born-on date." (http:www.nuvo online.com/97/08/07/street/street3.html).

Kinnaird Beverage Bodies & Trailers literature, various dates.

Bob Koprivica, Jr., interviews, various dates.

Liles, Allen. *Oh Thank Heaven! The Story of the Southland Corporation*. Dallas: Southland Corporation, 1977.

Mickey Truck Bodies literature, various dates.

"New Formula for Beer Distribution." *Material Handling Engineering* (October 1997): 43–46.

Canada. Department of Justice. *Report Concerning an Alleged Combine in the Manufacture, Distribution and Sale of Beer in Canada*. Ottawa, 1956.

Rock Hill Body Company literature, various dates.

Schlüter, Hermann. *The Brewing Industry and the Brewery Workers' Movement of America*. New York: Burt Franklin, 1910.

Shih, Ko Ching and C. Ying Shih. *American Brewing Industry and the Beer Market*. Brookfield, WI: W. A. Krueger Co., 1958.

Silver Book for 1954, The. Detroit: Cosgrove and Equipment Associates, 1953.

Swan literature, various dates.

"Transportation Update, 1996." *Modern Brewery Age* (Nov. 11, 1996): 14–18, 39–40.

Weeks, Morris Jr. *Beer and Brewing in America*. New York: United States Brewers Foundation, 1948.

Wells Cargo, Inc. literature, various dates.

Wood, Donald F. *Beverage Trucks 1910–1975*. Photo Archive. Osceola, WI: Iconografix, 1996.

———. "Bodies for Bottles and Brew." *Special-Interest Autos* 48 (1978): 42–46.

———. "The Driver/Salesman and his Changing Role." *Beer Wholesaler* 9, no. 4 (1976): 34–35.

———. "The Driver/Salesman's Role in the Movement of Urban Goods." *Research Issues in Logistics,* published by the Transportation and Logistics Research Fund, The Ohio State University, Columbus, (1975) pages 211–219.

Index

Index by Beer Companies and Brands

ABC, 39
Acme Non-Fattening Beer, 58
Aetna, 53
Alpen Brau, 19
Altes Lager Bier, 12, 100
Amos, 50
Amstel, 139
Anheuser-Busch, 8, 13, 14, 26, 28, 30, 32, 34, 48, 77, 137
Atlantic, 85
Atlas Prager, 88
Atlas Special Brew, 33
Augustiner brew, 51
Ballantine, 70, 105
Barmann's, 46
Bavaria, 10, 11, 136
Beamish Irish Stout, 139
Belgish Abdijbier, 138
Beverwyck, 68
Bevo, 28, 29
Birk's, 57
Black Horse, 68
Blatz, 125
Blatz Old Heidelberg, 49
Bohemian Pale, 86
Boston Ginger Ale, 59
Brading's, 70
Brew 66, 116
Buckeye Distributors, 92
Bud Light, 7, 132
Budweiser, 23, 29, 77, 82, 119, 133, 135, 137, 138
Burgermeister, 110
Burke's Ale, 63
Busch Bavarian, 124
C & L Edelbrau, 58
C. Pfeiffer Brewing Company, 12
C. Schmidt & Sons Brewing Company, 18
Carling's Black Label, 71, 92, 122
Cast Brewery, 19
Central Brewing Company, 12, 60
Champagne Velvet, 97
Chester Brewing Company, 15
Cleveland Home Brewing Company, 45
Cleveland Sandusky Brewing Corporation, 98
Clevelander, 45
Cold Springs Brewery, 15
Congress, 18
Consumer's Brewing Company, 36
Consumers Ale, 36
Coors, 75, 82, 91, 111, 118, 125, 127, 136
Corona, 103
Crown Brewing Company, 20
Dallas Brewery, 64
Dawson's, 73
Detroit-Bohemian, 27
Diamond Springs, 21
Diamond State, 88
Dobler Brewing Company, 14
Dominion Brewery, 45
Dommelsch, 141
Dow Old Stock Ale, 60
Drewry's Ale and Lager, 62
Duquesne, 67, 106
Dutch Club, 95
Eastside, 78
Edel-brau, 57
Erin Brew, 85
Extra, 44
F.X. Matt Brewing Company, 36
Falls City, 87
Falstaff, 77, 82
Feigenspan, 15, 41, 75
Fort Pitt, 86

Fox DeLuxe, 85
Fox Head, 6
Garden City Brewery, 18
Gast Brewery, 19
Genesee Brewing Company, 93
German-American Brewing Company, 24
Gettelman, 39, 103
Globe Brewery, 55
Gluek's, 36, 78
Goenner & Company, 76
Goetz Country Club, 79
Gold Bond Beer, 98
Golden Age, 51
Golden Brew, 56
Golden Glow, 62
Golden Hudepohl, 97
Grain Belt, 49, 65, 72
Grand Prize, 87
Green Seal, 38
Greenway Brewing Company, 54
Greenway's India Pale Ale, 54
Guinness, 32, 102, 107
Gunther, 92
Hamm's, 90 108, 110, 117, 135
Happy Days, 20
Hauenstein New Ulm Beer, 107
Heidelberg, 93
Heineken, 133
Hemrich Brewing Company, 74
Hoerber, 52
Hohenadel, 63
Hornung's White Bock, 47
Iron City, 95
Jacob Hornung Brewing Company, 47
JAX, 73
Keeley Brewing Company, 59
King's, 37, 59
Kingsbury, 84
Kips Bay Brewing Company, 24
Koehler's, 101
Krantz Brewing Corporation, 96
Labatt's, 7, 43, 69, 71, 81
Lion, 12, 40
Lone Star, 90
Louis Bergdoll Brewing Company, 17
Lucky Lager, 38, 66 115, 135
Maier, 25
Maltosia, 24
Manhattan, 72
Meister Brau, 20
Metz Brewing Company, 79
Michelob, 116
Miller, 7, 10, 17, 29, 91, 104, 113, 128, 129, 132, 139, 140
Miller Brewing Company, 58
Miller High Life, 8, 83
Miller Lite, 134
Milwaukee Brewery, 16
Minneapolis Brewing Company, 49
Mitchell's Premium, 84
Molson's, 87
Moosehead, 79, 115
Moosehead Dry, 135
Muehlebach, 94
Narragansett, 99
National Bohemian, 108, 117
National Breweries, Ltd., 60
New Life Pilsener, 76
O'Keefe's, 50, 66
Old Chicago, 123
Old Dominion Brewing Company, 131
Old Dutch, 96
Old Shay ale, 42, 86
Oldenberg Brewing Company, 130
Olympia, 116, 119
Oranjeboom, 140
Ortliebs, 61

P.O.C. Pilsener, 104
Pabst, 24, 32, 75, 112, 135
Pabst Brewing Company, 80
Peipp's Hollander, 22
Penn Pilsner, 31
Pennsylvania Brewing Company, 31
Perfecto, 22
Peter Fox Brewing Company, 85
Peter Hand Brewery, 20
Pfeiffer's, 83
Pickwick Ale, 46
Piels, 125
Poth's Extra Beer, 11
Primator, 18
Protiwiner Export, 17
Rainier, 61, 67, 73, 105
Red Dog, 131
Red Hook Brewery, 100
Redtop Brewing Company, 109
Regal, 98
Regal Pale, 89, 94
Reisch Brewing Company, 13
Renners Old Oxford Ale, 53
Resch's Pilsener, 54
Rheingold, 90, 102
Rubsam & Horrmann Brewing Company, 44
Ruppert Knickerbocker, 89
Ruppert, Jacob, 14
S . F. Enterprise Brewing Co., 16
Schaefer, 86, 120
Schlitz, 23, 35, 38, 59, 61, 64, 65, 118, 130
Schlitz Encore, 122
Schlitz Malt Liquor, 123
Schorr-Kolkschneider Brewing Company, 55
Schultz Brewing Company, 47
Seitz, 42
Sharps, 126
Sicks' Century, 105
Sicks' Select, 91
Silver Top, 106
SK Lager Beer, 55
South Side Brewing Company, 34
Stag, 89, 122
Stark-Tuscarawa Breweries, 21
Sterling, 48
Stoeckle Select, 88
Stroh's, 20, 66, 109
Sunrise, 69
Tally-Ho, 52
Taylor & Bate, 71
Trommer's Malt Beer, 80
United Brewing Company, 50
Utica Club Pilsener, 36
Valley Forge, 96
Wacker & Birk Brewing Company, 22
Weber Waukesha, 92
Wehle Mulehead ale, 59
White Eagle, 57
White Rose, 64
Wiedemann's, 95
Wm. Hartig Fine Beers, 23
Wm. Peters Brewing Company, 13, 24
Wooden Shoe Brewing Company, 74
Yonkers Brewery, 14

Index by Truck Model and Make (chassis and body)

Alco, 12, 14
American Body & Equipment Co., 73
Atterbury Model D, 15
Auto-Car Equipment, 10
Autocar, 72, 85, 99, 109
Chevrolet, 7, 32, 34, 38, 73, 75, 77, 82, 90, 105, 108, 110, 121, 127

Columbia electric, 8
DAF, 136, 139, 141
Dailey, 113, 114
Dart, 15
Diamond-T, 23, 38, 61, 64, 78, 82
Diamond-T Model 211, 57
Diamond-T Model 351, 57
Doane, 67
Dodge, 35, 48, 49, 78, 79, 83, 100, 109, 112
Dorris, 19
Fageol, 57
Federal, 58, 70
Ford, 29, 31, 38, 48, 65, 73, 75, 79, 82, 91, 100, 104–106, 109, 117, 118, 125, 126, 130, 134, 136, 139
Ford C-series, 111, 116, 117, 122–124
Ford Model A, 32
Ford Model AA, 32
Ford Model T, 28
Ford Model TT, 29
Freightliner, 119, 132, 135
Fruehauf, 6, 70, 74, 81, 87, 92
FWD, 23
General Body Company, 61, 65
GMC, 27, 30, 39, 49, 66, 67, 102, 107, 108, 110, 113, 119, 128, 130, 137, 140
GMC Sonoma, 137
Grabowsky, 12
Graham Brothers, 31
Hackney, 142
Heil, 39
Heiser, 73, 83, 86, 91, 105, 117–119
Herman, 102
Hesse, 110, 111, 118, 119, 121–125, 134, 142
Hewitt-Lucas Body Company, 14, 106
Horner, 20
Indiana, 50, 51
International, 39, 50, 51, 58, 61, 67, 71, 86, 89, 91, 107–109, 116, 118, 123, 125, 131–135
Kenworth, 61, 89, 135
Kissel, 15
Kleiber, 16
Kranz, 60, 83, 122
LaFrance Republic, 36
Leyland, 102
Mack, 13, 24, 40–42, 75, 83, 86, 129
Mack Bulldog, 24, 52
Marion, 108
Mark Body, 125, 127
Marquette, 13
Mercedes, 138
Mickey, 113, 117
Mitsubishi, 131
Moreland, 25
Omaha Body & Equipment Company, 79
Packard, 24, 29
Palmer-Moore, 18
Peerless, 14
Peter Wendel & Sons, Inc., 75
Pierce-Arrow, 20, 24, 26
Reliance, 61, 110
REO, 37, 79
Scammell, 32
Schacht, 20
Sterling, 24, 62
Stewart, 58
Stoughton Wagon Works, 80
Studebaker, 44, 62, 63, 67
Trailmobile, 89
Volvo, 139, 140
Wacker, 61
Walker Electric, 8
White, 6, 7, 17, 22, 18, 19, 21, 28, 33, 34, 36, 43–47, 52–56, 59, 60, 63, 64, 68, 69, 72–74, 76, 80, 81, 84–90, 92–98, 101–106, 109, 120
White Freightliner, 115
White Model 805 T, 71

144